Meditation

Utilising These Easy To Follow Meditation Scripts, One Can Quickly Acquire The Skill Of Mindfulness And Relaxation

(How To Meditate, Get Rid Of Negative Thoughts, Remain Calm, And Achieve Peace For The Rest Of Your Life)

Derek Andrew

TABLE OF CONTENT

Introduction..1

Meditation For The Relaxation Of The Body...26

Techniques Of Meditation That Are Simple To Perform..32

How Should One Begin To Engage In The Practise Of Meditation?............................41

Thinking About The Whole World......................44

Techniques That Can Help You Become A Better Meditator 54

Connecting Points With The Muladhara Chakra 63

Before Each Presentation To The Board, A Meditation Lasting Five Minutes..........................81

A Feeling Of Contentment And Joy.......................87

Meditation With The Purpose Of Concentrating On Feelings...92

Techniques For An Intermediate Level Of Meditation 98

Meditation With A Strong Connection 108

Hands-On Healing Session With The Raphaelite Work System 113

Eliminating All Traces Of Negativity................ 123

How May One Get Mental Tranquilly?.............. 141

Technique 3 Of Creative Meditation Is Called "The Time-Out." 156

Different Methods Of Meditation........................ 166

How To Deepen Your Spirituality Through Meditation And Mindfulness Practises In Order To Draw Nearer To Your Creator 174

Advice On How To Calm Your Mind And Take Pleasure In Living In The Here And Now 177

Things That Should Be Kept In Mind When Teaching Mindfulness.. 181

Chakra Of The Solar Plexus 191

Introduction

Dear reader, I would like to extend a warm welcome to you and express my gratitude for your interest in Mindfulness: Daily Practises for a Calmer and Sweeter Life. This book will provide you with an introduction to mindfulness and the inspiration you need to start incorporating mindfulness into your everyday routine.

As a result of my personal experience, I am aware of how beneficial this practise can be; specifically, it may result in a better sense of serenity, a decrease in anxiety, and an overall sensation of being more present. My aim is that by sharing my story with you, you will be inspired to seek out this practise for yourself.

Anyone and everyone is capable of practising mindfulness and experiencing its results, which include being more grounded and reducing the risk of getting carried away by one's emotions and ideas when these aspects of one's experience attempt to drag one down with them.

The practise of mindfulness will astound you because it will very literally alter the way you see the world.

The reality is that chances to practise mindfulness are continuously being presented to us by life. It is not necessary to make any purchases of gizmos, to engage in an exhaustive amount of study, or to conjure up the determination to learn any unusual new age skills. To practise mindfulness, all you need are your senses and a commitment to yourself, even if it's just a little one at start, to become more aware of your day-to-day existence and the moment that you are now in.

And there we have it; the conclusion! In all candour.

As was indicated earlier, I have direct experience with the positive and gratifying effects that mindfulness can have, and what I've included in this book are the practises that I've learned and faithfully used over the course of the last three years in my own effort to become calmer and more centred. I know from firsthand experience how good and satisfying mindfulness can be.

It gives me great pleasure to tell you about my experience.

My name is Amanda, and I work as a nurse, which is an employment that is both satisfying and demanding. It's like a weird mix of great and dangerous and tough and exhilarating and draining all at the same time. I'm also a writer, which, as you might imagine, is a lot quieter and stiller endeavour than working in a hospital emergency room. It requires a mental flip of gears to go from the fast-paced environment of the emergency room to the blank white page.

When I first began my journey into meditation and mindfulness, I had not yet joined the fast-paced world of nursing, but I was seeking for a solution to alleviate the nagging worry that I had been experiencing on a consistent basis, much like a low hum in the background. I found that meditation and mindfulness helped me do both of those things. However, it's not always simply static on the radio. At other times, it struck me like a Mack truck, leaving me with the impression that I was entirely defenceless and at its mercy. I was unable to do anything except suffer as my mind whipped itself into a frenzy. These ideas, which often took the shape of some kind of self-deprecating drivel, frequently made me feel as if I was being hopelessly suffocated by them.

I was able to shut out these sensations as long as I stayed busy and diverted myself, but when it was quiet, there was that nagging voice in my brain, picking apart every move I took and focused on errors from my past and anxieties about my future while disregarding the moment I was in totally. Because I wasn't paying attention to what was going on around me, I found myself adrift in stormy waters and unable to just be. On other days, I'd feel mentally drained just from the stress of having to cope with my rambling thoughts. Those days were rare, however.

Naturally, feelings, ideas, and even awful circumstances will all pass through our lives at some point. The only constant is change itself. That's the way life is. But I came to see that I needed a strategy to reduce the extent to which I felt powerless and the likelihood that I would let my thoughts to carry me away. When I looked back on specific periods of my life, I found that I recalled my concerns and fears at the time more vividly than the actual event itself. This bothered me since I wanted to remember the latter. I made the decision that I wanted things to be different.

I began with the basics.

I vowed to myself that I would sit quietly in meditation for at least five minutes on a daily basis. PemaChodron's "How to Meditate: A Practical Guide to Making Friends with Your Mind" and Michael Singer's "The Untethered Soul: The Journey Beyond Yourself" are two books that I just finished reading. These books were important to me because they showed me an alternative way to look at life, one that addressed both the difficulties and the pleasures of life and made it possible to deal with any kind of situation by practising mindfulness.

I quickly came to the realisation that a simple procedure might provide extraordinary outcomes.

I realised that the seas had begun to settle down and that a tiny weight had been taken off of my shoulders. There was no fanfare or feeling of revelation associated with this realisation. Between myself and the fear that I was experiencing, a very little gap opened up, and in that gap, I discovered that I was able to see the events that were transpiring in an objective manner. I slowly came to the realisation that I had the opportunity to choose a response that was superior than the one I would have selected in the past. A pause for you to get breath. In addition to this, I discovered that I had a rekindled appreciation for the simpler things in life. A pleasant exchange with a friend, the rustling of the leaves in the forest, and the sound of the wind in the trees all come to mind. All of this was accomplished by maintaining my practise and being as present as possible from one instant to the next to the greatest extent that I was able. And despite the fact that professional obstacles, personal issues, and other types of challenges continue to surface on a daily basis, I have constructed a framework and a foundation from which to observe these challenges, which not only gives me room to breathe but also space to be appreciative and centred while life continues to unfold around me.

I would want to explain this approach of mindfulness to you in a way that is simple, easy to understand, and simplified as much as possible.

This book will provide you with a concise introduction to mindfulness, an easy-to-follow guide to beginning a meditation practise, and eleven different mindfulness practises that you may use in your day-to-day life. You will find these sections separated into three segments throughout the text.

In order to get the most out of the advantages of mindfulness, I believe that the following is the most effective method to utilise this book:

1. CONTEMPLATE. Get into the habit of meditating every day. If you already meditate, that's fantastic! Maintain your pace. If not, there is no need to worry. A good starting point is five minutes every day. It's enough to make a difference and start seeing improvements, and it's a modest commitment to yourself and your new practise that you can expand upon anyway you see appropriate. It's enough to make a difference and start noticing changes.

2. RETAIN YOUR ATTENTION. Choose one of the mindfulness practises presented in s 3-13 and do all you can to include it into your routine as much as possible. Begin immediately. With the help of these practises for mindfulness,

you will be able to bring the presence and awareness gained through meditation into the light and incorporate it into your day-to-day life. If you want to, you can try a different one every day, but you can also stay with one for many days at a period to see if it starts to seem more natural and simple to include over time. You will feel a stronger connection to some of them than to others, but you should give them all a go because you could be surprised by what works best for you. The difficulty with them is that they seem straightforward and maybe even a bit stupid when you first look at them; they appear to be too straightforward to make any kind of impact. However, the cumulative impact of glossing over these straightforward facts from one instant to the next is what causes us to become caught up in feelings and ideas that are unrelated to the present situation, as well as our fears.

3. KEEP UP THE GOOD WORK! Continue to build on this. Observe the positive effects that are occurring. I didn't believe anything was happening to me other than a little sensation of relaxation, and I was pleased of myself for sitting every day for a few minutes at a time. Other than that, I didn't think anything was happening at all. Then, without any prior warning, BAM! It wasn't until my spouse brought it to my attention that I realised I no longer had anxiety whenever I was required to parallel park. Don't make fun of me! I am aware of how little this victory was, but it was the first of many smaller wins. It did not happen instantly, but once it did, there was no discomfort involved. Simply put. A brightening of spirit as well as the peeling away of layers that needed to be cast off. This is the benefit that it can provide to you. It

will take you by surprise, and you'll feel a sense of satisfaction knowing that you're doing something so beneficial for yourself.

That wraps things up, my good buddy! Set aside only five minutes each day to meditate, and begin incorporating one or two mindfulness techniques into your daily routine while you go about your activities. It may seem to be straightforward, and in a sense, it is; nevertheless, the challenge lies in keeping in mind to practise mindfulness. However, by educating you to remain conscious as you go about your usual day-to-day activities, these approaches will assist you in maintaining your practise and helping you to keep up with it.

There is neither a predetermined sequence nor specific criteria to adhere to. I want you to think of these strategies as components of a mental toolbox that you can use throughout the day no matter what the circumstances are. I want you to be creative with this, and I want you to apply the techniques anyway you feel most comfortable.

Keep in mind that there are no unbreakable laws or regulations. Simply allowing oneself to experience the uncomplicated satisfaction of being more alert and alive.

It is my deepest conviction that practising mindfulness may bring about a transformation in one's life. Through the simple act of being present, you may bring your thoughts into focus and open your heart at the same time. It is my belief that via engaging in this practise, you will feel lighter, more at ease, and ultimately happy.

I want to express my gratitude once again for your purchase of this book and for making the effort to take care of yourself in this way. Dear buddy, I pray that life treats you kindly and abundantly.

Have fun on your travels.

#1. Exactly what does it mean to meditate?

The practise of meditation is both an exciting journey and an opportunity to access the infinite knowledge of the cosmic consciousness that is always accessible to everyone of us. It is an inner journey in which one lets go of all of the senses, the bodily belongingness, and everything else that there is. It is like being swept away by the ocean without any preconceived notions or opinions, but still being able to take pleasure in the ecstasy of the present moment, experiencing the same sense of being clean and vibrant as we do when we are in the water. The practise of meditation entails doing no activity and being still. It has nothing to do with being able to concentrate. When someone is forcing himself to concentrate, they are not practising true meditation. One must let themselves be guided by the experience without forming any queries or making any evaluations. It is a space of experience that does not pass judgement on anything.

It is a subjective inner movement that truly cannot be put into words and must be experienced to be understood. In the state of complete surrender, it is obvious that no one can pinpoint the origin of the happiness that is experienced, but to tell you the truth, this is irrelevant. The only thing that counts is the events themselves; everything else is irrelevant. When it comes to meditation, there are a lot of thoughts that go through a person's head, such as what kinds of sentiments and emotions are experienced throughout the practise. But the reality is that meditation is not a process; rather, it is a condition in which there is no thought. The mind is the source of thoughts, feelings, and emotions. And the mind is the door that has to be shut during meditation sessions. If one's brain is still active, it is impossible to feel the happiness and delight that come from connecting with the all-pervasive or the cosmic oneness.

The core of mediation consists of just bearing witness to whatever is going on around you. Because we have been programmed from an early age to think, plan, and investigate, it may seem to others who are just starting out to be a challenging procedure. However, after you have been used to letting go of all the junk from inside, you may then start the real trip. When you meditate, you are on a trip in which you do not know where you will end up. In the material world, it is necessary to be aware of one's destination before setting off on a trip. On the other hand, in the spiritual world, both the destination and the amount of time it takes to get there are completely illusory since neither one of these things really exists.

A little warm-up is something that might be fantastic and good to do before commencing the real voyage. For example, taking a five-minute break from your job and letting your mind to completely shut down so that you become a silent witness to the ideas, emotions, and feelings as well as the tension and congestion that are occurring inside you is one technique. And then doing it gradually when sitting at home or maybe on a weekend when you're not doing anything else except practising quiet.

When a person is completely immersed in inner quiet, they are nevertheless able to carry out their daily activities such as chatting, walking, and eating with full awareness and without allowing the inner silence to be broken by any external stimuli. Therefore, meditation is not just the act of shutting one's eyes and becoming still for some period of time; rather, it is a journey that continues during each of the waking hours of each day and throughout the whole year. When you meditate, you are encouraging the stillness of your inner self and the awakening of your awareness of the ever-present cosmos, both of which carry over into the rest of your day. People often say that they meditate and feel fine, but as soon as they begin their daily activities, the stillness evaporates and they are left feeling worse than before. Therefore, what you are doing is not meditation.

It is not true that practising meditation excuses one from living their life, from their duties, or from their employment. This is a fallacy that persists in today's culture. Therefore, it is common for people to joke that in order to meditate, one must first finish all of their responsibilities in the world, and only after that can one engage in this pastime. In point of fact, the reverse is true. One must practise meditation in order to engage more actively in their lives and to have a more vibrant inner life.

In the environment we live in today, we often experience feelings of exhaustion and depletion of our emotional reserves. Because of our addiction to competition, which prevents us from properly establishing goals for ourselves, we are constantly faced with the experience of feeling pressured from the inside. It is time to put a stop to this and start recharging our batteries from the inside out. This problem may be solved by making an effort to go within, towards the centre of our existence. Furthermore, this does not need you to stop what you are now doing. You are free to do anything you choose, with the caveat that you should be sure not to lose your inner centering or your connection with the cosmic oneness.

One of the common criticisms that individuals level at meditation is that they are unable to maintain a state of deep concentration during the practise. As a result, sooner or later, they lose up on the practise entirely. I will tell you a tale from the Zen tradition because the Zen tradition is full of wonderful stories that have a profound spiritual meaning.

Once upon a time, a student sought the guidance of a Zen Master in order to learn how to meditate and to become an expert in the practise of meditation. He had been on the road for more than two months in his pursuit of this one-of-a-kind Zen Master who he had heard really positive things about. At long last, he arrived, and the Zen Master greeted him with open arms.

The student approached the Zen Master and addressed him as "Dear Master," expressing gratitude for having him take them on as a pupil. I am one who is really committed to the cause. There is still one inquiry that I would want a response to from you. Please respond. I am interested in learning how long it will take for me to become an expert in the practise of meditation.

A nonchalant response from the Zen Master was "about ten years."

The student continued by stating, "Well, in that case, if you would like I can practise your techniques for more than 16-17 hours a day, and then perhaps this can reduce the amount of time it takes to learn." If I go ahead and accomplish this, how much longer will this process take?

The wise old man said, "Perhaps twenty years, or even longer than that."

The moral of the narrative that was just told is straightforward: impatience and the incorrect estimation of time may stifle the development of the blooming of your inner being. And another thing that happens is that we get too connected to the outcomes and try to exert complete control over everything by establishing deadlines. It is necessary for us to understand that meditation is not an activity that takes place in the physical world and does not need timed objectives. However, it is an experience that is beyond time, attachment, and the ability to be mastered.

Your inner self is given the opportunity to blossom when you meditate, and as a result, you may experience a change not just in your energy but also in the way you think. As time is seen as just an object and one's attachment to it is released, there is a corresponding improvement in the quality of one's internal energy as well as their thoughts. Not only is meditation necessary for achieving inner calm and tranquilly, but it's also necessary for clearing out the accumulated junk of repressed feelings, ideas, and emotions that we all carry around with us. They may even be those who are passed down to us through our DNA and, at times, serve as constraints in our life. Through meditation, you may find that you are better able to clear away this clutter on all levels of your being. As human beings, we don't simply live on a personal level; we also exist on a communal level. The experiences that our parents, grandparents, and ancestors have had collectively, together with the environmental exposures that we ourselves have had, as well as the exposures that our prior generations have experienced, are all encoded in our DNA.

The general populace has the notion that the only things that need our attention are our own karma or the lives we've lived in the past. However, even our DNA, particularly the trash that's been sitting dormant in it, has to be freed as well. One must feel whole in their entirety, which may be accomplished by doing all of the things that have been outlined above. Even Zen emphasises detachment at every level of instruction. Even while the DNA component isn't discussed in great detail, they will still urge you to remain quiet while you observe all of your thoughts and feelings and let them go as they come and go.

This book devotes the majority of its content to meditations that are based on the concepts of the modality known as Family Constellations. This modality is concerned with removing the garbage from our DNA, creating harmony in our family tree, and re-establishing the flow of love both within the DNA and throughout the family system. The majority of the challenges we face in life can be categorised as patterns, and if you can see these patterns in the context of family constellations, you will be able to get a more profound comprehension of the reasons why certain patterns keep emerging in our lives. Your connection to your DNA will get stronger, and you will find yourself in a state of greater equilibrium, if you practise the meditations and movements of the soul that are described in this article.

Meditation For The Relaxation Of The Body

Locate a nice, quiet spot where you may sit comfortably and find a space there. Turn down the volume on the phone, and dim the lights. This is your opportunity to experience inner serenity and tranquilly, and you may do so by relaxing and unwinding at this time.

Put your hands on your lap and check to see whether you have enough warm clothing on. To begin, you should shut your eyes in a relaxed manner.

Inhale slowly and deeply, then hold that breath for a few seconds. Feel a little pressure on your chest, and let the air out of your lungs as slowly as you can.

Once again, inhale slowly and deeply, and then hold that breath for a few seconds. Slowly let the air out of your body.

Take a deep breath in and then out. Take a deep breath in and then out. Take a deep breath in and then out.

Relax and let each breath to carry all of your anxiety and worry away with it. Give your body permission to feel peaceful, and allow yourself to relax even more.

Take a deep breath in and then out. Take a deep breath in and then out. Take a deep breath in and then out.

You are now calm and at ease with both yourself and the people and environment around you.

As ideas that are calming come to your mind, slowly and softly breathe in and out.

Imagine that sense of calm permeating your whole body, starting from your brain and working its way down to every part of you.

Your forehead, temples, and face muscles should feel much more relaxed now.

Relax your jaws and cheeks, and gently let go of any tension you feel in the muscles that surround them.

Permit the sensation to go down to your neck and to penetrate deeply into the muscles of your body. You should now feel less tension in your shoulders. Take several slow, deep breaths to calm your muscles and relieve any stress or tension that they may be holding.

Give yourself permission to feel it all the way down to your arms. You experience a greater sense of ease in your arms, all the way down to your fingers. Take several slow, deep breaths to calm your muscles and relieve any stress or tension that they may be holding.

Permit the sensation to go to your chest, and then let it travel down to your stomach. Observe how your stomach moves up and down with each breath you take. Take several slow, deep breaths to calm your muscles and relieve any stress or tension that they may be holding.

The emotion should be allowed to flow to your back. As the feeling works its way up your spine, you should start to experience a calming sense. Take several slow, deep breaths to calm your muscles and relieve any stress or tension that they may be holding.

Give succumb to the sensation as it travels down your thighs and buttocks. Your thigh muscles, both behind and in front, are beginning to loosen up, and as a result, you should feel more relaxed overall. Take several slow, deep breaths to calm your muscles and relieve any stress or tension that they may be holding.

Permit the sensation to go down to your knees, then your calves, then your ankles, and finally your feet. Every inhale and exhale brings a sense of peace and relaxation to your whole body. Take several slow, deep breaths to calm your muscles and relieve any stress or tension that they may be holding.

Continue to focus on your breathing as you meditate for a few more minutes. At the same time, be sure to maintain a calm condition. Take some time to savour this sense of calm and relaxation inside you.

Give your thoughts permission to meander in this timeless and expansive setting as you rest. In the event that you become aware of any distracting ideas, you should just still your mind and concentrate on your breathing.

When you are ready to return to your waking state, slowly open your eyes and take a few deep breaths.

Techniques Of Meditation That Are Simple To Perform

Open-ended and closed-ended practises are the two primary classifications that may be used to describe any and all forms of contemplative activity. Open-ended practise is a kind of meditation in which you do not concentrate on any one item in particular but instead allow your mind to wander freely and pay attention to anything catches your attention. During a practise with a closed door, you choose an item of concentration and then concentrate your attention on that thing. In this , we will provide you with one practise that has a closed end and two that have an open end.

There are literally hundreds of different meditation practises available, but I've found that the simplest ones are the most helpful when I'm just starting out.

Being mindful Meditation Based on Breathing

You may unleash awareness by relaxing, unwinding, and opening up your body and mind with this really simple meditation practise. This is a contemplative practise with little opportunities for expansion. Work on the following to have some experience with it:

After you have finished working on the seven aspects of posture, you should set a timer for five minutes.

Because your breath serves as the object of concentration in this exercise, you will need to direct all of your attention to it.

Take a deep breath in through your nose, and while you do so, bring your attention to the way the air in your body moves and causes movement inside it.

Exhale through your nostrils, and while you do so, bring your attention to the process of how exhalation causes air to leave your body.

Maintain your focus on your breath and make an effort to merge with it.

It is possible that your mind may start to wander throughout the practise; if this occurs, gently draw your focus back to your breath and reassure yourself that you will take care of all of your other issues once the session is over.

You just need to do it a few times, and after a week of constant practise, you should be able to concentrate more on your breathing.

Be careful not to give up on the practise, and make it a habit to do it every day, even if just for five minutes. Increase the time spent on it gradually until you reach ten, fifteen, and ultimately twenty minutes. After some time has passed, you will notice that you are able to focus better on every work that you do and that you are able to thoroughly and quietly experience each moment.

Meditation on a Mantra

Another form of closed-ended practise, this one has you concentrating on a mantra rather than, say, your breath as the one before it did. The purpose of this exercise is to train your mind to think in the desired manner and to attract beneficial events to you as a result of your efforts.

Choose any aspect of your life that you feel may need some work and write a constructive recommendation about it. If you want more cash, say "I am wealthy and abundant." If you want to be happy, you may say, "I draw happiness towards me easily." If you are stressed out, say "I am calm." If you want more wealth, say "I am wealthy and abundant."

Choose any uplifting mantra you choose—it may be as simple as a single word like "hope," "peace," or "kindness," for example—and say it over and over again during the whole session. After beginning with a one-minute session of mindful breathing meditation, transition into chanting your chosen mantra for anywhere between five and ten minutes. It is possible that after a few days of doing this, you will experience feelings that are more pleasant, serene, and tranquil than you did before.

Meditation with No End in Sight

You are not obliged to focus your thoughts on anything in particular while engaging in this simple exercise.

Get comfortable in the contemplative posture you've chosen, and then relax your body and mind by thinking about anything that makes you feel better. When you are feeling better, give yourself permission to let your mind wander freely and concentrate on one subject at a time.

Allow your mind to travel in whatever way they want, from thinking about the ceiling fan to thinking about the vase that is sitting on the table to thinking about how your daughter smiled at you to thinking about why you don't feel happy in life; then, notice each idea very carefully.

This practise will help you to relax and clear your thoughts so that you can focus better. When you take some time to relax, things that have been bothering you will often come to your attention. This enables you to better recognise your issues and find solutions to them. Just keep in mind that you should give each concept the appropriate amount of time before moving on to the next one.

After each session, you should make it a habit to jot down your reflections as well as an assessment of how well you performed throughout the exercise. This will allow you to go through your ideas and investigate them more thoroughly. Keep in mind that practising on a consistent basis is necessary in order to get mastery over oneself.

Boaz, you are blessed

Boaz was a prosperous farmer and a relative of Naomi's via her husband Elimelech's side of the family. He was a wealthy and successful guy who had a lot of money. Boaz was able to enjoy authority and notoriety as a result of his money, as is normally the case when wealth is involved. He had a high social rank and was held in great regard throughout the community. During the period of the Judges, when everyone performed what was right in his own eyes (Judges 17:6), Boaz stood out as a holy figure. Because he had given his life to God, neither his money nor his great rank were able to corrupt him. He was a man of integrity who, had there been a competition, would have been a strong contender for the "Ideal Israelite" prize. After all, the mere meaning of his name, Boaz, which is power, hints to the splendour of his existence. He was revered like a king by the common people.

Boaz left behind a living legacy, which ensured that his honesty and influence were never called into doubt. He was a hero because he would save Ruth from the abyss of doom and act as her saviour, the dazzling knight in sparkling armour. His great-great-grandson, King Solomon, who was known for his wisdom, would later honour him by naming one of the two pillars in the portico of the temple after him (1 Kings 7:21). Everyone who came to worship in the temple was given a reminder of the importance of maintaining their faith and being obedient in their everyday lives by the pillar that Boaz had built. Every Israelite had no question in their mind that Boaz was a blessed and reliable character who was able to carry the weight of the concerns of the world.

A depiction of a good man who was blessed by the Lord to become a blessing for others may be seen in Boaz. He was an authentic descendant of Abraham. His uncomplicated adherence to religion and respect to the law would ultimately alter the direction that human history would take. He would be an outstanding choice to portray the role of the kinsman-redeemer. Therefore, the one who would save the world, Jesus, would come from Boaz's family tree. Boaz, who was an ancient ancestor of our Lord and Jesus' older brother, is also our spiritual inheritance and a model for faith. This is because Jesus is our Lord. We give thanks to God for the wonderful Boaz, as well as all the other saints in our life who are like Boaz.

How Should One Begin To Engage In The Practise Of Meditation?

Always keep in mind that the actual practise of meditation is quite brief, but the philosophy that underpins it is very extensive. The truth is not a method of boosting or lowering one's energy; rather, it is a state of mind. How you see and interpret the world around you. The act of preparing for meditation might be more challenging than the meditation itself.Because of this, the vast majority of individuals in our world are unable to practise the art of meditation. There is a lack of readiness on their part to extend their intellect. Because of this, Patanjali'sAshtang Yoga includes the concepts of yama and niyama in its teachings. Before we can begin the practise of meditation, we are required to adhere to these guidelines for self-discipline.

I believe that it is possible for a practitioner to begin his meditation practise by first reciting the holy word omkar. This is what I have come to believe. Take a few deep breaths, then as you let your breath out, repeat the mantra chnatomkar.

What exactly is the omkar?

The holy cosmic vibration known as Omkar may be broken down into its component parts—the syllables A, U, and M. The waking state of consciousness is denoted by the letter A, the dreaming state of consciousness by the letter U, and the profound sleep state by the letter M. Following the letter M comes the fourth stage of consciousness, which is known as turiya. Additionally, there are states of awareness that exist beyond turiya.Turiyatit,Brahmichetna, BhagwatChetna, and MahatChetna are their respective names. Therefore, there are other libraries to investigate than waking life, dreaming life, and deep sleep.

The enormous and wide path of expanding one's awareness is what this is.

Therefore, we all have the potential for tremendous growth on the inside. Kundalinishakti may be thought of as the power that is responsible for the expansion of our awareness.

Therefore, to begin meditation, one should go into a room by themselves, close the door, and chant the holy word omkar while thinking on the meaning and significance of the word.

Thinking About The Whole World

When you first start meditating, you won't only be inquisitive about yourself and your practise; you'll also be curious about the world around you and how it works. You might also try meditating on the earth, fire, air, and water. These are the four elements. You will realise that you cannot truly separate them when you focus on them; this is a fantastic illustration of how interdependent all of the things in the world are, and that includes YOU.

When you meditate on these components, you have the option of either bringing a physical element into the room with you or visualising a symbol that represents that element. You may do any of these things. You could find yourself wondering, "What does meditating on these aspects have to do with my goal of discovering happiness and tranquilly within?" The practise of meditating on these aspects helps you develop awareness not just of yourself, but also of the mundane world around you.

The following constitutes the four components:

Your awareness will be brought into the here and now if you are cognizant of your connection to the planet and the role it plays in your life. You will get the most out of your daily existence and sink your roots deeply into the body of the land if you do this. Meditation might help you feel more connected to life if you've been feeling detached from the world around you. When you meditate, try to conjure up mental pictures of the ground. This may be anything having to do with the natural world, such as grasslands, forests, or even bare rock.

Remember that you are mostly made up of water, since it is an essential component of your body. Water is very necessary for living things. In addition to this, it naturally corresponds to a person's moods and emotions, which, much to water, might be shallow, clogged up, or very clear. Therefore, while you meditate with the concept of water in mind, think about imagery such as lakes, waterfalls, rainfall, and seas, among others, and try to determine which kind of body of water most accurately represents how you are feeling. You might start your meditation session by placing a bowl of clear water in front of you. This could be an effective way to focus your attention.

Air is a non-visible component that still has a significant role. While you are meditating with the concept of air in your mind, attempt to conjure up mental pictures of things like a little breeze, a dust storm, or a whirlwind. Open your mind to the possibilities that come with change. The wind is a metaphor for a person's thoughts and ideas, which are similar to the movement of the wind in that they are never motionless and evolve through time. Your ability to constantly examine your thoughts will improve as you practise meditation. When you first sit down to meditate, you may find it helpful to start by burning an incense stick and observing how the smoke moves around the room.

Fire is a potentially destructive but also potentially curative element in the elemental warning system. Indeed, it has a wide variety of characteristics. It cleanses while at the same time consuming, it generates heat and light, it may be hazardous while simultaneously being necessary, and so on. You may find it helpful to begin your meditation by lighting a candle. Focus your attention on the flame while you ponder on its beauty.

Advice on Meditating

The following are a few pointers that will assist a novice in learning how to meditate and getting the most out of the practise itself.

To ease into meditation, begin by sitting quietly for about three to five minutes at a time. This may not seem like enough time to make a change, but it is surely enough time for you to sense a difference in the levels of stress that you are feeling right now. As you get more experienced, you will naturally be able to extend the length of time you spend meditating.

Get a grasp on the fundamentals of the practise of meditation. In order to get more acquainted with the practise of meditation, it is a good idea to familiarise yourself with some of the written material that relates to its history.

You should also make it a priority to educate yourself on the fundamentals of meditation. So many people have the misconception that the purpose of meditation is to concentrate on one thing in isolation from all other thoughts. Nevertheless, you will find success with meditation if your objective is to become conscious of the times when your mind wanders and to reorganise your thinking pattern so that it consists of more positive ideas.

Getting things done in the manner that you like is also very significant. You may get guidance from a meditation master, a teacher, a guide, or even the website itself. There are many people that can help you. Finding your own method of meditation is the most essential thing you can do, despite the fact that all of these things have the potential to be incredibly helpful. There is no need to change what you are doing if what you are doing is successful for you and there is no cause to change it if it works.

Maintain a consistent practise of meditating every day. Even if at initially you are unsuccessful, you should keep working hard since it will eventually pay off. Almost nobody will ever struggle through a whole session of meditation without attaining some level of achievement. If it is at all feasible for you, try to set aside some time every day to engage in the practise of meditation. If this isn't something that might happen, then you should try meditating more than a few times a week.

Always warm up with some excellent stretches before you sit down to meditate. Stretching the muscles throughout the body helps to relax them, which in turn makes it easier for you to sit still and experience the benefits of meditation.

You should devote a certain space in your home to meditation, and you should utilise that space for all of your individual meditation sessions. This is not the right place for you to sleep or do business in. When you meditate, it is a good idea to have many candles lit in the room that you are in and to have numerous candles placed up in the room.

Make sure that the time you have set aside for meditation is a time when you won't be disturbed in any way by anything else going on in your life. During your time spent meditating, you should make sure that all of your electronic devices, including your mobile phone, tablet, and laptop, are turned off and hidden from view. In addition to this, you shouldn't be bothered by any guests or the.

Go to a meditation class if you want to improve your practise and obtain advice from other people who are also meditating, or invest in some books and DVDs that you can watch in the comfort of your own home. Your practise may likely benefit greatly from all of these things, and they can also assist you in exploring more avenues and choices.

Altering some other aspects of your lifestyle will assist guarantee that you are able to relieve stress completely and should be one of your top priorities. Altering the foods you eat, the thoughts that go through your head, and the amount of physical exercise you get are all things that may help you rediscover your concentration and steer clear of stress. It is also a good idea to avoid caffeine (found in cola, coffee, tea, and other beverages) as well as alcohol, as all of these things have the potential to make one uncomfortable and anxious. If you are a smoker, it is in your best interest to give up the habit. If you give up smoking, you will not only experience a wide range of positive effects on your health, but you will also find it much simpler to meditate.

Techniques That Can Help You Become A Better Meditator

Advanced meditation methods strive to reach joy, serenity, psychic and healing skills, and oneness with the Divine. While most basic and intermediate meditation techniques are focused on relaxing the body, calming the mind, and enhancing self awareness, advanced meditation techniques attempt to accomplish all of these things.

Meditation experts like monks, spiritual mystics, and seasoned meditators are the ones who typically put these practises into practise. These meditation experts are able to concentrate on one subject for extended periods of time. Some people who practise meditation for long enough eventually develop telepathic and even superhuman skills, to the point where they are able to levitate. Masters of meditation often devote at least four hours every day to the practise of meditation.

Keep in mind that you must purge your body of any negative energy and toxins before engaging in any advanced meditation method. Asanas, often known as yoga poses, are one approach to achieving this goal. Stretching, squats, tai chi, and gentle aerobics are some examples of fundamental workouts that you may do.

Listed below are some more advanced tactics and approaches for meditation:

Meditation on the Kundalini — This kind of meditation is performed with the intention of reawakening the Kundalini energy, which is situated at the base of your spine. Kundalini is the key to unlocking one's full creative potential. You will become more creative and prolific after the Kundalini has awakened inside you, and you will most likely begin your path towards self-actualization at some point during this time. If it is not done in the right way, Kundalini meditation has the potential to be harmful. When doing Kundalini meditation, it is usually better to do so in the company of an instructor or a friend. In order to practise Kundalini meditation, you will need to ensure that your back is in an upright posture while sitting in a comfortable lotus or half lotus position. Put your hands together in front of your heart, close your eyes, and recite the mantra "OngNamo Guru DevNamo" three times. This mantra might be translated as "I make a promise to the Divine within." After you have finished chanting, bring your attention to your breathing while taking few deep breaths. Now, see yourself breathing from your spine, and while you do so, visualise an energy coming up from your spine and travelling all the way to the top of your head. Keep going like this for the next fifteen to twenty minutes. If you have a heavy head, this is a sign that the energy of your kundalini has already begun to rise. At the end of the first half hour, offer a brief prayer of thanksgiving.

Laughter Meditation: Laughter meditation is one of the most accessible advanced meditation methods; yet, in order to practise it successfully, you will need to have a high level of focus and the ability to exert strong mental control. It is not simple to simply laugh without their being anything to provoke it. Those suffering from worry and stress often turn to this particular kind of meditation for relief. It is even used as a treatment for clinical depression. You should stretch your muscles before beginning your laughing meditation session. Pull your arms high up over your head and clasp your hands together in a tight fist. Perform some facial exercises in order to loosen the muscles in your face. When you are ready, take a seat, and don't forget to smile. Smile broadly and start laughing as soon as you can. Rather of coming up with anything witty to say or think, simply laugh naturally. You need to make sure that your belly is the source of your laughing and that it has a deeper tone. Be conscious of your laughing, and just take pleasure in the now. You have 10 minutes to complete this task. After then, put an end to your laughter and shut your eyes. Pay attention to what you are feeling. What emotions do you have? Clear your mind and focus only on the sensations and emotions that you are experiencing in the present moment. Let go of any and all judgements you may have. Continue to heighten your senses and allow yourself to experience every breath, every movement of your finger, feel the breeze on your skin, and smell the aroma of the place you are in. Continue doing this for ten to fifteen minutes. You will notice substantial benefits in your emotions, feelings, and your life in general if you practise laughing meditation on a regular basis for a period of thirty days.

The Heart Seal Meditation Technique is one that allows you to be in one with your crystallised self. This technique may be found here. The process of crystallising your Self involves severing the connection between your ego and your Self and opening the centre of your heart. Crystallising your Self is the first step towards being one with the Divine, which already resides within you. Sitting in the lotus or half-lotus posture, with your legs crossed in front of you, is required for the heart seal meditation. You're going to want to close your eyes and focus on the area right in the middle of your forehead. Place your hands in a cross position over your heart, which may be found in the middle of your chest. Feel your heart beating slowly and gently. While doing so, tilt your sternum forward slightly and recite the mantra "Humee Hum BrahmHum" aloud and in a rhythmic way. Put your attention on the here and now and try to let go of any distracting ideas that may come to mind. This practise will help you become one with the Divine that already resides within you by allowing your mind to become empty. Continue doing this for at least half an hour, or even an hour if you have the time. Say a brief prayer expressing thanks just before we call this meeting to a close. Bless not just yourself but also those you love, those you consider friends, and even those you consider foes. Doing so on a regular basis can help you experience pleasure, develop compassion, and gain a deeper level of understanding. Before beginning each session of meditation, you need to warm up with some physical activity, as is the case with the vast majority of advanced meditation techniques.

The purpose of more advanced meditation methods is to help you acquire a greater level of awareness and improve your focus. Your relationships, as well as your ability to experience satisfaction and joy, may benefit from more advanced meditation. The vast majority of experienced meditators have already attained a higher state of awareness and have mastered the art of exercising dominance and command over their own thoughts. They possess great mental power, and some of them are even able to read minds and create profiles of individuals based just on appearance. More crucially, experienced meditators and mystics attain a level of bliss in which they are able to experience happiness despite the absence of any obvious cause for it.

Connecting Points With The Muladhara Chakra

In the instance of the first chakra, there is a catch when a person takes the stance that he cannot live without a person. This posture creates a problem. This is not an issue when it comes to parents and their children, but when it comes to adults, it is. This is due to the fact that the person who has taken on the role of "I cannot live without you" is feeding the energy of the first chakra of the person to whom it has connected up.

The common expressions "without you, I would die", "without your help, I have no livelihood to live", "without you, I would not survive", and so on are strong signals that there is a hook to the first chakra that you need to sever.

Activation of the MULADHARA chakra with various exercises

You will find a variety of exercises of varying types below, and it will be up to you to choose the ones with which you are most at ease. You are free to repeat these steps as much as you want and even mix them with the previous ones.

Chromotherapy is grabbing a bright red cardboard or sheet and staring at it intently for a short period of time (no more than five minutes, so that your eyes do not experience any strain). While you are looking at the cardboard, you need to pay great attention to how you are feeling, if anything comes to mind, etc. while you are doing so.

Healing with stones is what gemmotherapy, sometimes known as gemmotherapy, is all about. In this scenario, the best course of action for you would be to acquire one of the stones associated with the first chakra, which are listed in the tab located above. Following that, you should take it into your left hand and then close your palm around it. Take as much time as you need to picture a brilliant red energy pulsating out of the stone you've selected and travelling through your whole body until it reaches the first chakra in your system. When you go there, picture yourself clearing anything that may be soiled or plugged up and cleaning it all up as you go. At the conclusion, notice how the light emanating from your first chakra illuminates the area at the bottom of your spine.

In the practise of Mantra Yoga, the mantra that corresponds to the first chakra is called the LAM mantra, and it is pronounced laaaaaaaammmmmmmm. You may do it as many times as you like in a day, but be sure to have a personal notebook where you record what you experience, how you feel, and what you recall while you are doing it.

When it comes to aromatherapy, individuals who are pressed for time may find it most beneficial to make use of the essences and incenses that are specifically designed for each chakra. You may have a look at the information page to get a better idea of the scents that can help you cleanse and activate your first chakra. at this scenario, you should fire the incense or the essence at a location where you will be able to quietly absorb its perfume.

Music therapy: In this instance, the issue is whether you should listen to music associated with the first chakra for a short period of time (or for as long as feasible). This might be the sounds of nature, such as a jungle or birds, or it could be an ancient piece of music with a lot of drums and loud noises, like the African Muladhara Chakra.

The Muladhara farm, according to the teaching of the Orientals, is located two fingers on the anus and two fingers under the genital organs, (base of the spine or coccygeal bone); consequently, the enlightened clairvoyants of the East claim that said farm has the brilliance of ten million suns; however, I must note that this farm is also known as the church of Ephesus that is mentioned in the Apocalypse of St We are now dormant, waiting for the time of waking to arrive so that we may climb the spinal cord and unlock the remaining chakras, which will then offer us light.

The Kundalini is the holy fire of the Third Logos; it is an electronic solar fire that resides in the electrons, and the flames of the heart govern the ascent of the Kundalini via the spinal cord. For this, they need a great deal of merit, merit in the heart, (the cultivation of virtues), the wise meditating on the Kundalini, devotees worshipping him, and in households where the ideal marriage prevails, he works with him literally. The Gnosis that was revealed by Master Samael Even Weor, the Avatara or messenger of the present aquarium age, contains the information that is necessary to build it.

If we want to know the qualities that are necessary to open each of the churches or farms, we need to study the book of the Apocalypse of St. John in regard to the churches of Ephesus, Smyrna, Pergamum, Thyatira, Sardis, Philadelphia, and Laodicea. There, we will find a description of the requirements for entering each of the churches or farms.

It is important for you to understand that whomever opens the first Muladhara church or farm has control over the earth element. After that, the elementals of this element serve the magician, and the magician has the ability to either produce or halt tremors. It is vital to see, particularly and in a self-conscious manner, everything we see and imagine; it is required to wake up our awareness if we want the powers of

Being. It is imperative to eradicate from our perceptions all of the subjective parts. It is essential to perceive especially and in a self-conscious way everything we see and imagine.

The human being is composed of three distinct parts: the body, the soul, and the spirit. The soul acts as a mediator between the spirit and the body. We are aware that the soul is housed in a magnificent body known as the astral body, and that this organism has a set of senses that are located inside itself. The best clairvoyants tell us about seven farms, and Mr. LEADBEATER explains them in exquisite detail; these chakras, which are essentially the astral body's senses, are described by Mr. LEADBEATER with the utmost elegance. These magnetic centres are situated in close proximity to the glands that are responsible for the production of internal secretions.

The first, or root, chakra

The root chakra is the first of the seven primary chakras and is located at the base of the spine. But don't be fooled by this; in order to raise their spiritual being, a person must first have an open, healed, and balanced root chakra. You can't strive to improve your spiritual being otherwise. In point of fact, you need to look at each of the chakras in this manner. In other words, prior to attempting to open or heal the higher, more spiritual chakras, you should concentrate on healing each of the lower chakras in turn before moving on to the upper chakras.

If you make the error of attempting to open your third eye or crown chakra before you have opened and balanced the lower chakras, it will either not function at all or it will lead to major difficulties of a spiritual and mental nature. If you want to avoid these issues, you should avoid making this mistake. It is possible to undergo emotional trauma and terrible experiences if you have a third eye awakening or try other spiritual routes, such as a kundalini awakening, before you have completely developed your spiritual potential.

It is essential that you begin with the basics when you are just beginning anything new. This is analogous to consulting a medical doctor or any other kind of specialist. Would you want a doctor who bypassed studying anatomy and went right to doing brain surgery? I wouldn't think so. Not at all, of course. The same is true for your own personal growth on a spiritual level. In order to proceed, you must first lay a solid foundation for the body, mind, and soul. The root chakra is the place where this foundation is established.

The capacity to feel comfortable and secure in the material world is connected to the root chakra, which is most strongly linked with Mother Earth. This chakra is located at the base of the spine. The ability to satisfy our fundamental need of having a place to sleep, food to eat, and protection from harm is related with a balanced root chakra. The energy level of this chakra is considered to be lower than that of the other chakras, which is reflected in the colour red associated with it. However, nothing in the human experience can be divorced from the spiritual aspect of existence, and as a consequence, having a blocked root chakra may result in a wide variety of emotional and mental symptoms.

Maintain an Inquisitive Attitude

Do you remember when you were young and you had an insatiable need to learn all there was to know about everything? This is the mental attitude that you need to maintain even as you get older and become an adult. Always remember that there is something new to learn. When you reach the point when you believe you know all there is to know about a topic, it is time to stand back. Even when it comes to skills that you currently have, there is always more that can be learnt about them or that can be polished with practise.

When interacting with individuals from a variety of backgrounds and ways of life, there are a number of additional scenarios in which this will be useful. It's possible that you're working with someone who has a fixed point of view that you find to be too restrictive. Or maybe you have the presumption that your environmentally conscious coworker is completely ignorant about life. What makes you think that till I ask more questions and look at it?

Everyone has a unique upbringing and experiences the world through a lens that you most likely do not share due to the differences in experiences that people have. As you go further into learning about the peculiarities that other individuals possess, you will also get a fresh perspective on who you are as an individual. In the end, it will make it easier for you to comprehend other individuals.

Increase the depth of your understanding

The greatest method to get a deeper understanding of individuals is to challenge them using more careful reasoning. Questions that are intellectually challenging or even offensive tend to be the ones that lead to the most intriguing findings. When we discuss topics that the vast majority of people do not bring up in their day-to-day encounters, not only will we get more knowledge, but we will also perhaps see this individual in a new way.

You may put this into practise with members of your family, customers, or even coworkers. Not only will these discussions build your connection with them, but they will also provide you with a deeper understanding of individuals hailing from a variety of backgrounds and walks of life. The important thing is to never believe that you have reached your full potential in terms of personal development or intuitive abilities.

Develop a heightened awareness of the specifics.

When an intuitive person gets more in touch with the environment inside themselves and around them, there is no question that they will be able to pick up on additional signals that will assist them in being even more deeply connected. This is because these cues will serve as a bridge between the intuitive person and the environment. The encouragement of this physical activity may be shown in a few different ways.

To begin, you have the option of sitting in a room by yourself. This may be a location that you've been to before, or it could be somewhere completely new. Take some time to yourself, find somewhere to sit where there won't be any interruptions, and focus on seeing the room in its entirety. Look out for the things that aren't immediately visible, even if you believe you already know all there is to know about the area you're in.

Your eye will become more attuned to new happenings and even changes in energy as a result of this training.

An other method is to create a simple mental image in your head, which you can then use to help you. It might be anything as simple as a coloured dot or a form that only exists in two dimensions. When you are initially getting started, you should make an effort to keep your attention fixed on the target for at least fifteen seconds, or even longer if you are able to. Your mind will be conditioned as a result to not cycle through as many ideas, to slow down, and to become more present in the here and now.

You should begin to add form to your shape in order to create a three-dimensional object as soon as you are able to continuously hold this picture in your mind for the fifteen second increment. To take the activity to a higher level, try visualising the item rotating in your mind's eye and adding more specific details. After you have completed this step, reduce the amount of time you have to a half minute.

This practise is designed to educate your eyes to extract more information from the environment around you. Following consistent practise, you will be able to acquire information very rapidly, which will be of great use to you when reading individuals and the situations in which they live. It is also possible that it will benefit you in circumstances in which you may need to think extremely quickly.

Before Each Presentation To The Board, A Meditation Lasting Five Minutes

First, ensure that your headphones are properly plugged in. Naturally, you should choose just the music that will put you at ease. You do not want to listen to anything that will thrill you in such a way that it will prevent you from being able to meditate, such as hip-hop.

Step Two: You should adjust the volume of the music so that it is just right; however, you should be careful not to make it too loud since doing so will make it more likely that you will get distracted. You do not want to turn it down so much that you have to concentrate on the music that is being played, but at the same time, you do not want it to be too loud either.

Step Three: Be careful to breathe as normally as possible during this whole process. You may find it helpful to inhale deeply and slowly through your nostrils, pressing the tip of your tongue softly against the roof of your mouth as you do so. Then, instead of exhaling through your nostrils, you should exhale through your lips, which should be slightly parted.

Step Four: You will discover that ideas enter your head at random intervals from time to time. It is imperative that you shift back your attention to the music that is now being played in the background. You need to make sure that all of your feelings are involved in that music that is playing, and that you love it to the very depths of your being. In fact, you should be so concentrated on the music that is playing that you give yourself up to it fully.

Step Five: As you continue to allow yourself to resonate to the beautiful music that is being played, you will notice that your breath and your heartbeat progressively synchronise to the 'pulse' of the music. This will occur as you continue to allow yourself to resonate to the music. This indicates that you have arrived at the "entrainment point," sometimes known simply as the "point." Your state of mind is congruent with the state of mind conveyed by the music that is being played and is also heading in the exact same direction.

You could find yourself in a position where you have to resolve a major disagreement at work at some point. In these kinds of circumstances, it is quite simple to let one's sentiments of annoyance and rage take over, both of which have the potential to be significant roadblocks when it comes to completing a task. Let's have a look at a straightforward meditation that just takes five minutes and may assist us in resolving that inner struggle.

A short meditation of five minutes designed to help you cope with conflict in the workplace

First, you need to sit quietly with your eyes closed and give yourself permission to experience all of those conflicting sensations without judging them in any way.

The second step is to cultivate a feeling of compassion and empathy inside yourself, in addition to a profound sense of thankfulness for the things you currently possess. While you are doing this, keep your attention on your breathing and try your best not to let the feelings of anger or fear that are running through your head as a consequence of the conflict in your mind that has not yet been resolved distract you.

Step Three: enable the sentiments of love and compassion to flow through you, and then give yourself permission to enable those feelings to spread to other people as well, even those with whom you may have a disagreement. After you have emerged from your meditative state, taking this precaution will help guarantee that you do not make the issue any more difficult than it currently is. This meditation that is focused on 'feeling' will guarantee that you perceive things in the most non-judgmental manner possible, helping you to make the most sensible choices possible.

It is of the utmost importance that your mind is completely de-stressed when you get home from work. If it is not, you will bring all of the unnecessary emotional baggage from your place of employment into your home, which is something you most certainly do not want to do because it will end up destroying your inner peace as well as the inner peace of the people you come home to. When you get home from work, it is most important that your mind is completely de-stressed. Let's have a look at a very efficient five-minute meditation that will help you relax after a long day at work, giving you the opportunity to feel revitalised so that you may enjoy the remainder of the day to the fullest extent possible. It is truly something that you are able to perform most effectively since all it requires is for you to go under a shower– which is something that you most surely do when you get home from work regardless of the circumstance!

A Feeling Of Contentment And Joy

One of the nicest things about meditation is the fact that it is effective. Happiness in its purest form is attainable, and you can get there by making an effort on your own. Since it is common knowledge that one must go inside themselves to find genuine joy, the only thing necessary to accomplish the goal of achieving happiness is to focus on improving oneself. You don't have to be miserable in order to provide joy to other people; rather, the more content you are, the more you have to give to those around you.

This is the very reason why meditation is beneficial for everyone and why it may be considered an act of love. You are able to attain a higher level of being via meditation, which not only frees you from the urge to search for answers in the outside world but also makes it possible for you to lend a hand to others who are in need.

Meditation is a practise that may educate you to respect aspects of yourself that are deserving of that regard. These aspects include your desire for true happiness, which is unwavering and risk-free in every way, as well as your confidence in your capacity to achieve pleasure through your own efforts.

Having to contend with pressure and anguish

The primary impetus behind my decision to start meditating was an urgent desire to reduce my levels of stress. I had gotten to the stage in my life when it appeared to take over everything, and I had to deal with it. Because of that, even my performance at work was beginning to deteriorate. At first, I wasn't certain that meditation might help, but then I realised that giving it a go couldn't possibly do any harm.

Although it won't completely alleviate your anxiety and pain, meditating may definitely help you cope better with them. You don't have to fully commit yourself to a new way of life though, which is another option. Even if you just follow a few of the fundamental components, you will see a significant difference.

When you find a solution to your issue of anxiety and anguish, it is only natural that you will be the one to profit most directly from its resolution. However, there are others who feel the same way. This is due to the fact that you become less resilient when you subject yourself to unnecessary anxiety and anguish. You lay responsibilities not just on yourself, but also on the people around you: both in that you have to rely on them for aid and support, and also in that you damage them with the dumb things you could do or say out of weakness and fear. You place these loads on both yourself and the people around you. You, on the other hand, have too many issues of your own to be of much use to them with their difficulties, which prevents you from assisting them with their issues. If, however, your mind is able to learn how to quit producing stress and suffering for itself, then you are less of a burden on other people and are in a better position to provide a helping hand to those who need it.

Meditation With The Purpose Of Concentrating On Feelings.

1. Get started with the breath meditation and do it regularly.

2. When you are ready to begin this meditation, you should shut your eyes even if you are practising the breath meditation with them open.

3. When you are ready to start this meditation, focus your attention on a particular feeling that you are now experiencing anywhere in your body.

4. Once you've decided the feeling you'd want to concentrate on, put all of your attention on that one experience.

5. Take note of the characteristics of the experience, including the following: a. Isit consistent and unchanging, or does

its strength fade away or change over time?

b. How does the feeling physically manifest itself? Is it vague, distinct, or tingly?

b. From what source does the feeling originate?

d. Where does it end up after it disappears completely?

6. While concentrating on the experience, make an effort to refrain from passing judgement on it. Try not to classify it as either pleasurable or bad in your mind. In addition, there should be no resistance created towards the experience, nor should any attempt be made to regulate it. Your only responsibility is to be aware of it.

7. Maintain your concentration on the experience, or shift your attention to another sensation.

Meditation as a means of concentrating on one's thoughts

1. To start, make a habit of doing breath meditation.

2. When you are ready to begin this meditation, you should shut your eyes even if you are practising the breath meditation with them open.

3. When you are prepared to start this meditation, direct your focus to the ideas that are running through your head.

4. You should never pass any kind of judgement on your own ideas, and you should never try to reject or exert any kind of control over them. Just relax and let them to enter the realm of your consciousness as they want.

5. Pay attention to the characteristics of your ideas, specifically:

a. Do your ideas remain constant and undisturbed throughout time, or do they gradually fade away or shift in terms of their level of intensity?

b. From what source do your ideas originate? Where do they end up after they disappear completely? Are you able to locate this location?

6. At this point, focus your attention on a single specific idea. Keeping an eye on it with your attention as it travels across your range of awareness is a good idea. Continue to watch it till it disappears. What do you notice in that split second between when one idea leaves your mind and when the next one starts to form?

7. Focus your focus on the space that occurs between the many concepts in your head.

8. What are some of the characteristics of this area? Is there calm or is there commotion? Is it a static image or a moving one?

Meditation as a tool for concentrating on feelings

1. Get started with the breath meditation and do it regularly.

2. When you are ready to begin this meditation, you should shut your eyes even if you are practising the breath meditation with them open.

3. When you are ready, direct your focus on an emotion that you are now feeling.

4. Under no circumstances should you pass judgement on your feelings, nor should you make an effort to fight or suppress them in any way. Just relax and

let them to enter the realm of your consciousness as they want.

5. Pay attention to the characteristics of your feelings.

6. Do your feelings remain constant and unalterable throughout time, or do they wane with time or change in terms of their intensity?

7. From what sources do your feelings originate? Where do they end up after they disappear completely? Are you able to locate this location?

Techniques For An Intermediate Level Of Meditation

It is common practise to instruct beginners to concentrate and become aware for a relatively little amount of time, anywhere from five to ten minutes. Those who are just starting out are given an introduction to mindfulness and mental training. Intermediate practitioners, on the other hand, are able to engage in longer sessions of concentration, mantra, and creative meditation, for example twenty to thirty minutes. Although it can seem simple, maintaining your concentration on a single idea, word, or area of your life for twenty to thirty minutes at a time can be rather tough. Because of this, it is recommended that only practitioners who are already at the intermediate level keep practising for an extended length of time.

The following is a list of meditation tactics and practises that are appropriate for practitioners with intermediate levels of experience:

1. Paying Attention Make it a habit to become more self-aware by paying attention to your feelings. Paying attention to all of the feelings that you are experiencing in the present moment is yet another method of mindfulness meditation that you may put into practise. This is a method of mindfulness that is intermediate in difficulty.

In order to put this into practise, you will first need to locate a quiet space in which you can meditate. Take a seat, either on a chair or a cushion. Spend some time bringing your attention to your internal state of mind. Feelings may be described as "joy," "sadness," "anger," or "disappointment," for example. Always keep in mind to categorise it without passing judgement. Do not criticise yourself for experiencing negative emotions such as sadness, anger, or disappointment. It's sufficient to just recognise all of those sensations before moving on. Spend around five minutes every day engaging in this activity.

If you tend to let your emotions get the best of you, you should try this strategy. Your sentiments and emotions will be easier to manage with the aid of this strategy. It will assist you in developing a greater sense of detachment from your sensations and emotions. Daily practise of this might last anywhere from fifteen to twenty minutes.

2. The Cravings Control Meditation Technique This technique is for intermediate practitioners who have achieved sufficient self-awareness and control over their thoughts in order to use it effectively. This method is often used in addiction support groups and treatment facilities, such as Alcoholics Anonymous and other similar organisations.

To do this, you will need to choose a chair that is comfortable for you and concentrate on being aware of your impulses. Do you have the impulse to eat excessively all at once? Do you find yourself hankering for a glass or two of anything alcoholic? Do you feel the desire to consume drugs that might hurt you or that are illegal? Label the cravings as you become more aware of them, and then let them pass without passing judgement on them. Instead of giving in to the temptation or want, focus on the hope that it would go away. At the first sign of a destructive impulse, gently redirect your attention to an affirmation that the urge will eventually pass. People who are fighting an addiction to alcohol or drugs may make use of this incredibly effective method to help them break free of their dependency.

People who desire to enhance their sensitivity to distractions while simultaneously strengthening their willpower might benefit from using this strategy. Daily practise of this might last anywhere from fifteen to twenty minutes.

3. Guided Imagery: This meditation method is also known as guided visualisation, and it is often used by yoga practitioners after they have completed the asanas, which are the poses that make up the physical component of yoga. During guided imagery, you will often be doing meditation or yoga under the supervision of a teacher who will direct you to envision soothing images such as a white light, a beach, or a forest. This will help you clear your mind and prepare for the practise. The widely held belief in psychology that there is a strong connection between the mind and the body serves as the foundation for guided imagery. It is predicated on the idea that everything you can conceive of

in your mind may be experienced by your body as if it were real.

Imagine every aspect of an orange, including its hue, consistency, peel, and aroma. This is an example of one of the most fundamental types of visualisation methods, which psychologists and medical specialists employ to explain this concept. After then, the physicians will ask you to imagine what it would be like to smell and taste an orange. If you do this, you will notice that you will experience the same tingling sensation as you would get while eating a real orange. This is because the two sensations are identical. This provides irrefutable proof that your body perceives something that is just in your mind as being real.

The primary purposes of guided imagery are to reduce feelings of tension and to relax the body. This kind of meditation is also employed by a significant number of people who study and practise the law of attraction.

4. Mantra Meditation - There are a lot of different ways to meditate with mantras. One of the most well-known forms of meditation is called Transcendental Meditation, and it is used by a large number of famous people and successful businesspeople.

To put this strategy into practise, locate a supportive chair or a cushion and sit there. You could try closing your eyes and taking several deep breaths. First, bring your attention to your breathing, and after you've done that, start reciting a mantra in your head. You may say the word "love" or "peace" over and over again. The Sanskrit phrases "Baba Nam Kevalam" and "Love is all there is" are often chanted by meditators who have reached an intermediate level of practise.

When engaging in this method, you are required to concentrate wholly on the mantra. Bring your attention back to your mantra if you find that your mind is wandering or you find that you are thinking about meaningless things. When you are ready to wrap up the meeting, take a moment to offer a brief prayer of thanks. This kind of meditation is appropriate for intermediate practitioners and may be practised for a total of 40 minutes, twice daily.

Studies have shown that these procedures do not have any affects on a person's mental state, physical state, or psychological state at all. These techniques are safe to use in general. It doesn't matter where you do it—at home, at a yoga studio, on the beach, or in your garden—you'll get the same benefits.

Meditation With A Strong Connection

This session of guided meditation will assist you in reestablishing your connection with the universe. It is recommended that you meditate on a daily basis in order to see major improvements. Make an investment in your mental health, your sense of calm, and the relationships you have.

Try to find somewhere peaceful and comfortable to spend your time. Relax in a comfortable position, either sitting or lying down. Take a full breath and hold it for twenty seconds. Straighten out your back to allow your breath to come in a more natural way.

You have twenty seconds to shut your eyes gently as you focus on being aware of your breathing.

Take a long, deep breath in and then gently let it out. Take a minute and a half to breathe deeply three times. Give your body permission to relax and become used to the new breathing pattern. Feel how your body is becoming more at ease with each breath you take.

Maintain a focus on the here and now in your consciousness. Imagine there is a light on top of your head; you have complete control over the colour of this light.

Imagine that this light is surrounding your whole body, from your head all the way down to your feet. Take a deep breath and count to ten. Imagine that this light is a manifestation of your connection to the otherworldly realms. Take a full breath and hold it for twenty seconds. Next, see that light becoming stronger. Imagine that from this light, multiple angels appear around you and begin to minister to you. Your imagination may go wild as you consider whether or not they have wings, whether or not they have a face, and whether or not they have a form that can be identified.

When it comes to creativity, there is no such thing as right or wrong. Imagine for a moment. Hold your breath for twenty seconds. You are now connecting with your spiritual mentors and guides, who are constantly by your side but want your permission to intervene in your life and bring about good change directly. Although they are always there for you, they are unable to do so until you give them that permission.

Take a moment to pause, focus on your breathing, and Bring enlightenment and love that is not conditional. Imagine for a moment that you open the door for these creatures of light to come into your life and help you. ... so that they may direct your course and your steps in the direction of all that is the will of the divine for you. Keep deep breathing for the next twenty seconds.

Give them permission to bless your heart, which will help heal any scars, awaken your inner light and divine flame, remove any negativity from your journey, and protect you at every step. They will assist you in living a life filled with pleasure and lightness as well as everything else that your heart desires. Take a deep breath in and then out. Imagine that the angels who are all around you are coming up to you and offering you a present. To fully appreciate what you are experiencing at this very now, let your imagination go wild.

This gift is a symbol of the qualities that your spiritual guides believe you lack, including love, light, bravery, and forgiveness.

Experience the significance of this gift to you. Take a full breath and hold it for ten seconds. You should express gratitude, and you should try to keep the present close to your heart.

It is impossible for him to disappear. Keep in mind the lovely present he gave you, and he will come to your aid when the time comes. Now there is a much stronger connection between you and your mentors. They have come to help you find balance throughout your journey. Everything will turn out well in the end.

Be conscious of the fact that the more your connection to the universe, the greater the likelihood that good things will occur in your life. Take a few deep breaths and begin to move your body in gentle circles as you savour this pleasurable feeling to the fullest extent possible.

Hands-On Healing Session With The Raphaelite Work System

A pre-session interview is conducted at the beginning of a Raphaelite Work healing session. The purpose of this interview is to orient both the client and the practitioner to a location from which to begin the session. The Raphaelite Work practitioner will perform the treatment on the client while the client is fully dressed and laying on a massage table or a futon on the floor. The Raphaelite Work practitioner will put their hands on certain locations on the client's body that are related to the elements of earth, water, fire, air, and ether. During the treatment, the client will remain completely clothed. The purpose of bringing up these things is to facilitate a discussion of any experiences, ideas, or sentiments that may come up. After the Hands-on Healing session, the client will participate in a post-session interview. During this time, the practitioner will assist the client in integrating the knowledge gained from the five domains, observe how the energy is moving, and identify any changes that may have taken place within the domains.

- A Healing Session Conducted Individually Using the Raphaelite Work

A conversation between the client and the One-on-One facilitator that centres on the client's relationship to her or his experiences in each of the five domains is started. Within the context of a one-on-one session, the client will experience a healing presence that will lead to the development of clarity in her or his awareness of self and her or his connection to others. The One-to-One facilitator will utilise breath and inquiry to create an environment that is soft, non-directive, and non-judgmental. This will be accomplished by listening from the facilitator's heart, demonstrating love and compassion, and enabling the client to feel comfortable. The facilitator does not provide advise or comments to the client, nor does he or she get personally engaged in the process that the client is going through.

- The Work Retreat of the Raphaelites

A Raphaelite Work Retreat leader will lead participants through an in-depth exploration of the language and flow of energies in each of the five domains during the Raphaelite Retreat, which provides time and space for participants to be alone with themselves. The activities of daily life are put on hold for the duration of one's stay at a retreat, during which they are assisted in focusing their attention inward. The Raphaelite Work Retreat offers participants a better degree of mental acuity with which to cope with the challenges of day-to-day living by strengthening and extending the connection between themselves and their lives. through engaging in activities involving one's breath and present, as well as through working within the framework of the five domains, one may cultivate a new sense of self and discover new sources of delight.

Although a retreat of at least five days is encouraged, shorter retreats of varying lengths are also possible to organise.

2. Meditation on Loving-Kindness and Compassion

This Buddhist practise, which is often referred to as metta meditation, entails not just focusing sentiments of compassion and kindness towards oneself, but also towards other people.And if I may go so far as to say it, to every living thing as well. This meditation has a quality that is not only very pure but also unconditional and altruistic.

Research has shown that practising loving kindness meditation raises levels of pleasant emotions, which in turn lowers levels of negative emotions and even alleviates some of the symptoms of depression.

This meditative state that "does good" also reduces chronic pain, provides relief from severe migraines, and encourages a sense of belonging, all of which contribute to improved health and feelings of pleasure. What a fantastic thing!

Even if someone warns you that it's not a simple practise to follow, you should still give it a go. We are all more than capable of loving one another and showing that love to one another. As a consequence of this, you may start to see that anytime we show compassion, it is returned to us in like. Kindness, empathy, and compassion are important traits to cultivate as you go about your everyday life. Observe the bad behaviour of others around you to see whether it results in any changes. Also, try not to pass judgement on either yourself or other people.

A word of caution: the practise of loving meditation has the potential to become apparent via the operation of the law of attraction. It is possible that you will be taken aback if, soon after you begin the practise of loving meditation, the very same person who is on your mind when you are engaging in the practise contacts you out of the blue.

At a minimum, you should sit in meditation for three to five minutes. At some point, you could get to the point where you want to go for 10 minutes, or perhaps half an hour, if not for a longer period of time. It's a heady and hearty experience all the way through.

How to go about it

1. Ensure you are wearing clothes that is comfortable and does not impede movement.

2. Assume a seated or reclined posture, whatever affords you the greatest degree of ease.

3. Loosen up your body and your posture. It is recommended that you shut your eyes.

4. Bring your attention to either your heartbeat or the solar plexus chakra, which is located in the middle of your belly.

5. Find inner calm and love for the person you are. Take pleasure in it.

6. Repetition of three or four encouraging phrases, such as "May I be happy, May I be safe, May I be healthy, and May I be strong," or any other words that make you feel good in the present time, is the sixth step.

7. Exhale deeply and force all of the tension, negative thoughts, and self-

doubt out of your body with each exhalation.

8. As you breathe in, sense love emanating from your solar plexus, and focus on the feelings that you are experiencing.

9. Grant yourself the right to be joyous, free, powerful, and at peace with who you are.

10. Direct your one-of-a-kind statements towards your family, your friends, another individual, and anybody else you can think of.

11. Send love to particular individuals or to whole nations that may be going through a difficult time.

12. Observe this practise of meditation throughout the duration of the time you have assigned to yourself, as well as until you experience feelings of thankfulness and compassion.

13. As soon as you emerge from this meditative state, give some thought to what has just taken place. Stretch out your muscles, and go out with love in your heart. Give yourself a nice stretch.

Eliminating All Traces Of Negativity

I had no idea that the solutions to my problems lied inside myself when I set out on my quest to find happiness and to find a way to cope with the amounts of stress that I was required to deal with on a daily basis. Because this Lebanese thinker had a very creative way with words and was able to help me realise where I was going wrong in my life, one of my lessons was provided to me via the works of Khalil Gibran. This lesson was given to me because it was one of the things that I learned. My body was giving out under the strain. My daily existence was filled with negativity, and that negativity was a part of who I was. I had a lot of unfinished business from the past, both in my professional life and in my personal life, and I appeared to be clinging to it as if it were the most important thing in my life. This was true for both aspects of my life. Your mental processes are always going through the situations that have caused you pain or worry. This might include harbouring resentments or feeling dread when you don't believe you can achieve something, both of which are common occurrences in the job. When people are cruel to one another, even if you don't suffer any bodily injuries as a direct result of their actions, you may as well since the patterns of thinking that result leave a permanent mark on who you are.

Take a look at the quote that is above, and although though it may not make much sense to you right now, it will develop into something that you will completely comprehend once you see that all of the misery that you have been through has been the result of your own beliefs of how life should be. Your supervisor has been unfair to you and has given you an excessive amount of work. Your lover has been unfaithful to you. Because you've been hurt so badly in the past, you're afraid to move on to the next stage of your life. There is always going to be something that is going to hold you back, and you never really perceive that it is something that is not external. You are so immersed in the negative energy that you are unable to notice anything else outside it. I can still vividly recall thinking about how poorly I was treated at my place of employment. I recall going to bed each night fervently hoping that some type of fortunate opportunity would present itself to me, but what I discovered through my practise of meditation was that it is not a matter of chance. It is just your perspective that makes you feel less than you should when you see someone who has all of the qualities that you want but do not have. In a similar vein, when you experience negative emotions such as rage, worry, or tension, the reality is that it is your own perspective that is the cause of these feelings.

People who struggle with low self-esteem often discover that, although their condition may have been triggered by criticism, the manner in which they responded to the criticism is what ultimately led to their struggles. You are better able to put events in their proper context and go with your life when you meditate regularly. I used to think that it was something that only those who had a lot of spare time performed, but through my personal practise of meditation, I've discovered that it's not quite as straightforward as I once thought. Yes, you do need time to learn how to meditate; but, if you actually break through that barrier that lies between your anxieties and your happiness, you will begin to recognise that the time spent meditating is only a tool towards being a better person rather than the end goal in and of itself. That is all there is to meditation. It is not for those of high social standing or an independent attitude. It is available to everyone, even those whose wounds do not seem to be able to be healed. A good buddy of mine came to me a few years ago with issues that felt insurmountable at the time. She had reached the breaking point due to her level of anxiety. She was unable to go beyond the negativity in her life, and as she dumped all of her baggage onto me, it seemed to me that she needed a guide to assist her in moving beyond all of that negativity and into a more positive place in her life. She was able to work her way out of the rut that she had gotten herself in with the aid of the notes that I had written for her.

It was not an overnight process, but I used the notes that I wrote for my friend as the basis for this book because, if you were to meet her now, you would see a self-assured, very happy, and balanced human being who, like me, had taken the journey into meditation and who had found that it does not matter how many scars you bear from the past. This book is based on the notes that I wrote for my friend. They do not constitute the whole of who you are. The only thing that makes a difference is how you choose to live your life, and if you want to rid yourself of negativity, meditation is a practise that may assist you in doing so.

The destructive forces that are working against you

When you allow yourself to entertain unfavourable ideas, you allow a piece of your identity to dissolve. When you first start meditating, one of your goals should be to become conscious of the unpleasant aspects of your life and to remove those aspects from it.

It may seem to be common sense, yet harbouring unfavourable thoughts completely nullifies any possibility of experiencing joy. Therefore, as we go through the exercises in the s that follow, we place an emphasis on positivity. Additionally, it is essential to make an effort to evaluate your life and figure out what unfavourable aspects of your life cause you to feel stressed, sad, or even depressed. Let's take a look at some of the problematic aspects, since you really need to be aware of what they are before you can try to get rid of them. Because when you meditate, you concentrate your mind on things other than the negative, the effect of which is that you will view life from a new perspective and be able to find a positive spin on any given situation: Meditation can assist you a great deal to achieve this because when you meditate, you focus your attention on things other than the negative.

Negativity, dread, depressed thoughts, envy, rage, fear, and spite are all examples of negative emotions.

All of these things are rather clear in their unfavourable nature. When you are preoccupied with negative feelings of any kind, there is less place in your head for positive feelings to exist. You need to become aware of your emotions and determine the origin of your worries because, unless you do so, you won't be able to make any progress towards resolving them and will be unable to consign them to the past. Before we teach you how to meditate, you should make an effort to recognise the unfavourable emotions you are experiencing by writing them down. It's possible that you'll experience fear. In the space next to the word fear, write down the reasons why. It's possible that you won't be able to adequately describe some of the terrible emotions you're experiencing, but you'll be able to identify the sensations anyway. The practise of meditation is beneficial to you in a significant sense because it enables you to move farther away from all of the detrimental influences that are present in your life. Just for a moment, put yourself in the position of being stuck on a standing stone in the midst of a river. It is impossible to go ahead or backward since there are no other standing stones. Right now you are in this location. Through meditation, you will be able to gain some distance from that stone and make your way to the beach, where you will have a plethora of options available to you. Think about the things in your life that are not positive. Whether it's rage, envy, or worry that's getting in the way of your happiness, meditation may help you recognise these emotions for what they really are: obstacles to your joy that need to be overcome before you can really be content.

Meditations with Movement

In the conventional sense, learning how to do moving meditations might be a bit more challenging. During this kind of meditation, your body will be moving, but your mind will remain motionless. This condition could be reached by engaging in a particular activity, such as singing or dancing, for example. If you are feeling frightened or humiliated in any manner, the only possible explanation is that you are aware of other people and that your mind is busy. Most of the time, moving meditations may be defined as any activity in which you find yourself into a flow state or a state of intense relaxation. I said before that I feel that travelling slowly on a scooter may be a type of meditation for me. This is true for me. However, it may be anything from learning to play the piano to enrolling in a class in Brazilian jujitsu. Once again, we are able to understand how simple, organic, and straightforward Zen is. You are practising meditation even if all you do is set aside some time for activities that put you in a relaxed condition. There are some individuals who may need to figure out what it is for them, but everyone can discover a kind of movement meditation that works for them. Even as you are moving your body, you may have to force yourself to keep your thoughts quiet. When you are walking or engaging in some other activity, the mind is often not as concentrated or engaged as you are aiming for; yet, what you are actually seeking for is a flow state of meditation. It is certainly an improvement over doing nothing, but it is in no way a flow condition.

Take in a Tai Chi performance given by a Taoist grandmaster. This is an example of how movement meditation may be practised. However, one cannot learn to dance just via mental practise. It is not something that can be learned simply using your intellect. You get into a zone where everything comes easily to you. Taking someone by the hand and moving around the dance floor with them is the most effective method for teaching them how to dance. By doing so, their body really becomes in touch with the dancer who has more expertise, and this happens on autopilot with no input from the brain at all. It is simple to botch any kind of singing or dance routine. Your brain just has to wonder, "What will I do next?" for you to completely botch the situation. Because, similar to other types of meditation, movement meditation does not need input from the brain, which is something that has a tendency to disrupt the natural flow. Chi Gong and Yoga are two examples of well-known forms of movement meditation.

A stroll in the woods or a stroll by the shore.

Standing shoulder to shoulder with the practitioner and breathing in and out is a Chi Kung practise that is both straightforward and very efficient. Raise your hands over your head as you take a deep breath in. Raise your hands to your waist as you exhale gently and deeply. And as you are doing so, make an effort to feel the energy in the palms of your hands. There is no need in worrying about or overthinking the procedure, especially in regard to where you should place your hands. You will notice, when some time has passed, that your hands are in harmony with your breath, which is in sync with your thinking. If you do this twice a day for a total of six minutes, you will notice an improvement in your energy levels and ability to concentrate throughout the day.

Another simple method is to go for a stroll on a beach, gaze down at your feet, and concentrate on the sensation of the sand and the water passing through the space between them. Sensitise your senses to the bond that exists between your feet and the earth. This is a very powerful method for calming the mind and staying in the here and now. A lot of individuals live too much of their lives in their own thoughts. As a result, it is much simpler to let go of one's ideas and bring one's attention and energy down to one's feet, where it may then be combined with the additional sensations of the sand and the water.

It is beneficial to blend stillness with movement throughout one's meditation practise. Although they are both forms of meditation in the sense that one's thoughts are brought to a halt, the benefits gained from each are distinct. People have a tendency to enter contemplative states of mind while they are engaged in activities such as painting, gardening, vacuuming, or digging holes. Because if you attempt to do these tasks in a short amount of time, it is simple to perform a poor job, and you will fairly rapidly find yourself going nuts as a result. Patience and the attitude that "it will get finished when it's finished" are necessary components of an effective approach to finishing these projects. Mostly due to the fact that they are so dull. A few more thoughts on the practise of meditation.

IF MEDITATION MAKES YOUR BODY FEEL UNCOMFORTABLE, STOP DOING IT. If you only sit for 15 minutes a day on average, then sitting for two hours straight is not a good idea for you. Start with 20 minutes of meditation each day and build up from there. Start with 5 minutes if you find that 20 minutes is too much. Exerting oneself beyond your natural limits is not a Zen practise since it goes against nature.

There are no restrictions on attaining enlightenment, Kundalini, Divine Amrita, or any of the other spiritual states that are eagerly sought after. Every person is different, and some achieve significant milestones on their very first day. Everyone is different, therefore you should choose a solution that works for you.

The finest things in life, like Zen meditation, breathing clean air, and attaining enlightenment, are ones that don't cost anything and are simple to do. Have fun with the procedure.

How May One Get Mental Tranquilly?

If you look up the word "peace of mind," the dictionary will tell you that it refers to "a feeling of being safe or protected." On the other hand, I agree that "the absence of worry" is a more precise description of happiness than the American one. Achieving a peaceful state of mind in spite of one's surroundings and conditions is the goal of this practise.

The realisation that you are in control of your mind, including your ideas and the way you react to the actions of others, is the first and most important step towards achieving inner tranquilly. You will never be able to live in peace so long as you refuse to accept responsibility for how you respond to the acts of other people. Therefore, the moment you come to terms with the fact that you are in charge of how you react to other people and the circumstances in your life, you can begin to make progress in this area as an alternative to being controlled by the things that are happening around you.

In order for you to continue to enjoy mental tranquilly, the following are some recommendations that might assist you in maintaining your attention.

Acquire the skill of practising mindfulness meditation.

In the event that you have been hesitant to try meditation since you do not consider yourself to be "spiritual," then you should be aware that scientific research are now being conducted that return the advantages of meditation. A study conducted in 2018 and titled "Cognitive Ageing and Long-Term Maintenance of Attentional Improvements Following Meditation Training" is a good illustration of this. The study claims that, "The existing learn about is the first to provide evidence that intensive and persevered meditation practise is related with enduring enhancements in sustained attention and response inhibition, with the conceivable to alter longitudinal trajectories of cognitive alternate throughout the lifespan." This is just a fancy way of saying that the research used to be demonstrating that meditation increases your brain's capacity to concentrate both in the now and in the future.

Although there are many who do meditation for spiritual reasons, this is not an essential function of the practise. The advantages to one's body as well as one's emotions are something that anybody and everyone may take advantage of.

You will learn how to be in the here and now by doing mindfulness meditation and being familiar with its core principle. Because of this, you'll be able to push away the anxious and bothersome ideas that keep popping into your head. It helps you get some control over anxious feelings and tension. This gives you permission to ride in peace despite the fact that not everything in your lifestyle is ideal. And there are a plethora of advantages to the body.

Reduce the amount of time you spend on social media.

There are certain things about social media that are accurate; yet, there is a significant body of research that demonstrates the ways in which social media may be detrimental to the mental health of its users. The usage of social media often prompts us to evaluate the highlights and lowlights of our life in light of the highlight reel that our friends and family are posting. This may be a healthy and productive exercise. Your life's messes will by no means be able to compete with the bright points that other people are expressing about their own lives. In the meanwhile, if you are having trouble finding serenity and you often find yourself comparing yourself to others based on what they post on social media, it may be best for you to abstain from using such sites.

The use of social media is another source of distraction. It satisfies our FOMO (fear of missing out) appetite in a satisfying way. With access to social media available on our mobile devices, it is easy to be tempted to stop what you are working on or thinking about in order to "check" what is going on with friends and family members. This may be a challenge for those who are trying to be productive.

Put the past in the past.

When one allows oneself to get preoccupied with events that had place in the past, it becomes difficult to maintain focus on the here and now as well as the future. When we concentrate our attention on things that we cannot change, we make it difficult for ourselves to maintain mental composure. If there is anything that can be improved upon in the prior, then you should work to do so. Anything other than this indicates that it is time to forgive others, forgive yourself, and go on with your life.

Try not to take things too personally.

When you let things go and don't let them bother you, maintaining mental calm is much easier to do. And if you are the kind of person who is easily offended by the slightest thing that another person does or says, you are doomed to live in a never-ending kingdom of frustration. You won't be able to feel in control of your thoughts, and you won't have any serenity for very long. However, if you choose to focus your attention on seeing the best in other people, you will be able to shift your thinking in a way that will make finding peace a great deal less difficult.

Pick and choose your conflicts with caution.

If you make it your public mission to correct every individual who is doing anything that you don't agree with, you are going to be in a continual state of tension because you are always trying to change the behaviour of other people. In addition to this, it will be quite difficult to keep your thoughts concentrated on the thing that you would want to be the primary focus of attention. You like to do the same component with the people and situations you confront on a daily basis as you are taught to do when dealing with your children, just as parents are trained to choose their fights with their children.

For instance, you may now not agree with a discussion that is taking place between your colleague and your supervisor; yet, if you are not a part of the conversation, it is best for you to stay out of it. If you choose to keep yourself in check, you are putting yourself in a situation where you will have to select a side, maybe even putting your career on the line, and introducing stress into your life that you would rather not have.

Make it a priority to keep a diary.

Writing in a journal is an excellent method for releasing the ideas that are occupying too much space in your head. You may release all of your worries and concerns after you have written them down, at which point they will no longer be in your thoughts. Be aware, however, that some individuals find it helpful to physically destroy the paper by tearing it up or burning it as a sign to show that they are moving on from those ideas.

Writing in a journal may also assist you in processing difficult experiences and gaining a new perspective on familiar subjects. In addition to that, make sure you take the time to write about your day, do research based on it, and go on from there.

It doesn't matter how hectic your life may seem to others, you should always make an effort to carve out time in your calendar for moments of peace and quiet.

Being distracted and unable to concentrate are both side effects of living a life that is always chaotic and full of activity. This does not imply that you should avoid people at all costs; nevertheless, spending some time to isolate yourself from other people and just be silent might be beneficial in assisting you to mend fences with your internal monologue. If you realise that you no longer have any serenity in your life, you can benefit from going on a retreat by yourself. You have the option of going away for the weekend by yourself, or even just for the day. Find a place with some peace and quiet to reflect. Give yourself permission to speculate on the thoughts that have been running through your brain recently. The next step is to work up a strategy for addressing such ideas. Give yourself permission to rest and rejuvenate during this time period.

There are moments when it might be challenging to realise what we are thinking and how the thoughts that we are considering are influencing us. If you are having trouble achieving mental tranquilly, you may find it helpful to consult with a therapist in your area. They are aware of the appropriate questions to ask in order to help you get to the bottom of the problem you are having. Then, they will be able to provide you with actions that you may do to help you find serenity and maintain it.

How to Get Ready for Your Meditation Session

If you want to get the most out of your meditation practise, you should be familiar with the following guidelines first:

Take an Inventory of Your Current Self

You need to set aside some time to reflect on who you are and the principles that guide your daily life. You may start by taking an inventory of your life as it is right now. Start by examining the way in which you are now conducting your life. Is everything turning out the way you envisioned it? Take a close look at the life that you have fashioned for yourself. Have you zeroed down on what really interests you? Do you put forth too much effort? Figure out which aspects of your life are most important. Think about the things that are most important to you. Taking stock is comparable to organising one's closet. You get to choose what you want to preserve and what you want to get rid of in this scenario.

Find Out Where You've Been

The journey that is life is often used as a metaphor. Make use of this concept as you get ready to meditate so that you may examine your life in more detail. You may scribble down how far you have come in life, or you could design a map instead. Both options are available to you. You are able to include significant milestones in your biography, such as friends, family, and significant events that have occurred in your life. Now, ask yourself this question: has it been a difficult slog uphill all the way or has it been smooth sailing? If you do this before you truly dedicate yourself to a meditation practise on a regular basis, it will help you become more aware of the direction you want your life to go. Keep in mind that we all leave traces in the past; thus, do not be frightened to look back at the tracks that you have left. If you want to realise where you are in life today, it is essential to take a look back at where you came from.

Keep a log or a diary.

Additionally, it would be beneficial if you kept a meditation diary for the purpose of serving as a record for yourself. Consider each post in your journal as a photograph that will be added to an album that you will be able to browse over and reflect on in the years to come. You should keep a record of the many types of meditations that you have attempted, as well as make a note of how each one went and whether or not there were any difficulties along the road. It is recommended that you make it a routine to take down some notes immediately after each meditation session, since this is when your thoughts are considered to be at their most clear and your memory is at its most recent. But keep in mind that you should simply scribble down brief notes. Do not force oneself to keep a notebook or make it a duty to do so.

It Is Time to Begin Our Journey

It's possible that once you've spent some time taking stock of your life, planning out your path, and reminding yourself to write things down, you'll feel like you're ready to start learning how to meditate. It is now time to make the first move and start over in your life; the moment to act has come. The decision to begin meditating marks a significant turning point in one's life. It is a fresh approach to the future that will lead to a higher understanding of one's own life and of the world around them.

Technique 3 Of Creative Meditation Is Called "The Time-Out."

Because of the frenetic nature of life, it may be difficult at times to carve out some time for oneself to rest and decompress. This simple method, which won't take you more than a few of minutes to complete, will provide you some concentrated downtime just when you need it the most.

Find a spot where you won't be disturbed, and then sit comfortably on a cushion on the floor or on the edge of a chair, maintaining a straight spine. Imagine a circle drawn on the ground around you at around the same distance as an arm's length.

Imagine that this circle suddenly starts emitting a dazzling white light. Observe how it rises up around you and eventually becomes the shape of a cone, with you seated in the midst of it. You are shielded from the pressure and anxiety that comes from the outer world by this cone of bright white light. While you are there, you should experience utter tranquilly. You are in a secure location, and you may unwind now. Take as much time as you need to reflect on this picture.

Take a few slow, deep breaths, and then open your eyes in a gentle manner. Take with you throughout your day the feeling of safety and calm that this moment gave you.

Technique 4 of Creative Meditation: "The Countdown"

You can improve both your ability to concentrate and the amount of time you can pay attention to anything by using this strategy. Additionally, it has the potential to be a helpful one in getting you to sleep at night.

Find a spot with less noise, or you may carry this out while laying in bed. You are going to want to close your eyes and begin counting backwards from one hundred to one. When you realise that you have lost track of the count and are thinking about anything else instead, start again at one hundred and count down from there. It is normal for you to realise that you are slipping into ideas repeatedly; try not to become irritated about it. The development of attention and focus is the target of this exercise; reaching the goal is not the point of the practise.

Continue this practise for a certain amount of time (a minute or two, or five, or if you're using it to assist you go asleep, until you have really fallen asleep if that's your goal).

5. "The Inner Smile" is the name of the fifth creative meditation technique.

This is an effective method for fostering a greater sense of acceptance and love for oneself.

Begin by placing yourself in a sitting posture (either on a cushion on the floor or on the edge of a chair) in a location that is both peaceful and secure and one in which you will not be disturbed.

Take a few slow, deep breaths and try to maintain a smirk on your face while you do so. Imagine a location between your eyes and a little bit above them, which represents the opening of your third eye. Imagine that in front of your third eye there is a glowing golden sun that is hovering in the air.

Imagine that the light from this sun is beaming into your third eye and travelling all the way around your head. You should feel it glistening and flooding your mind with golden light as it does so. Imagine that this light is pure golden love, and it is travelling all the way around your head, past your lips, which are still in that small grin.

You should feel the golden love light travelling down your neck, passing through your chest and abdomen, surging down your arms, and pouring out of your hands. Feel it go from your chest all the way down to your legs, then into your feet, and finally out into the earth.

Feel this magnificent golden energy rush through you, erasing any negativity, any ideas that you no longer need, and anything else that isn't serving you in any way. Sense it being removed by this light and absorbed into the soil.

After you have completed everything, sit quietly with your eyes closed and take several deep breaths. During this time, focus on the sensation of golden energy shimmering all over your body. Open your eyes in a slow and gentle manner, and carry this sensation with you as you go about your day.

Method 6 of Creative Meditation: "The Sweeping Breath"

This is a kind of breathing meditation that is said to be beneficial for giving one with energy.

While seated comfortably, pay attention to your pulse for around 10 counts, and then take a few long, slow breaths.

Take a long, deep breath in, then as you let it out, picture your breath travelling all the way through your body, beginning at your head and ending at your feet, before disappearing into the ground. Visualise any extra tension or stress being carried out of your body and into the ground together with your breath as it travels downward.

Repeat this expansive breath a few times, releasing any energy that has been trapped and any stress that has built up into the soil.

Now picture a gorgeous golden light enveloping your whole body and creating a shimmering effect around you. Imagine taking in this light and letting it permeate every part of your body as you breathe it in.

Before opening your eyes, make sure you have a minute or two to sit in silence first.

Method 7 of Creative Meditation Is Called "The Walkabout"

This method will not only help you calm your racing thoughts; it will also assist you in stretching out your muscles and joints. This walking meditation draws its inspiration from the Buddhist tradition. In contrast to the other types of meditation, this one requires you to move about rather than remain seated.

You might practise this kind of meditation in a public place like a park or field, or you could even do it in your own backyard if you have one. You may also do it indoors, for example by walking up and down a corridor or across a room; but, doing it outdoors might be more pleasant. The aromas in the atmosphere and the many noises around you might amplify its influence.

To begin, you should stand with your feet about hip-width apart and your weight spread equally over both feet. Tune into the ground underneath you and become aware of the ways in which the earth provides you with complete support. You should look at the ground around 10–15 metres in front of you and choose a location on the ground to loosely concentrate your eyes on. Raise one foot gradually, starting with the heel. Take things slowly and methodically, planting your heel first, followed by the centre of your foot, and then your toes as you go forward. Carry on walking in this manner, putting one foot in front of the other, and getting a feel for what it feels like to move. The ground that you are standing on. The noises that are audible in your immediate environment.

If you notice that your mind is wandering off into thought, you may find it helpful to keep telling yourself, "lifting foot... moving foot... placing foot" as you take each stride.

When you have reached your destination, gently turn around so that you do not throw off your concentration, and then go back the way you came. Continue for a certain number of "laps," or for a predetermined amount of time (ten or twenty minutes is a suitable target duration), or until you feel as if you have reached the end of your meditation, whatever works best for you.

Carry the calm with you as you go on with the remainder of your day.

Different Methods Of Meditation

There are thousands of various ways to meditate, and each one may help you achieve the stillness and inner peace that you've been searching for. All of these distinct methods may be grouped together under a total of five distinct primary headings. These classifications are as follows:

Meditation on the Art of Concentration

Meditation on Being Present or Mindful

Meditation on Creativity

Meditation on Self-Reflection

Meditation that Is Focused on the Heart

The majority of individuals, and especially novices, turn to concentration meditation as a means to assist them relax and reduce tension. Let's take a look at each of the several approaches to meditation that are available.

Meditation Methods That Focus On Concentration

The practise of all other forms of meditation is made possible by first mastering the concentration meditation technique. When you have developed your capacity for mental concentration to such a degree that you are able to overcome any and all distractions and concentrate clearly on a single subject, you have achieved a state known as "flow." Our mind is tremendously strong, but it is often disorganised due to the fact that it is always thinking about a myriad of various things. You will be able to make your mind more strong and set yourself free when you are able to completely submerge yourself in the mental state in which you are able to block out what you do not want and bring in more good ideas and feelings. Concentration meditation is one method that may be used to assist in the reduction of stress in one's life, as well as the accompanying feelings of concern and anxiety.

Meditation with full awareness

The next style of meditation that is most often done is called mindful meditation. When you meditate with awareness, you are able to focus more intently, resulting in a stronger connection to and comprehension of the wonderful things that exist in the world. Your ability to enjoy the world and all that it has to offer is directly correlated to your level of success in practising mindful meditation.

Meditation on Creativity

People who desire to reduce the amount of stress in their lives might get benefits from practising creative meditation as well. When you practise creative meditation, you open yourself up to the possibility of actually feeling the marvels of love, admiration, gratitude, and compassion towards other people. After you have completed this process of meditation with success, you will have a greater knowledge of those incredible feelings that we all experience on the inside. These characteristics will all of a sudden spring to life inside us, helping to develop us intellectually and physically while also allowing us to create stronger connections not just with the people we love but also with the world around us.

Meditation on Self-Reflection

Meditation on reflection enables us to train our ideas and bring them under control. Reflective meditation gives you the ability to refocus your attention on the issue at hand whenever you notice that your thoughts have wandered off subject. Those who are going through a stressful time may benefit by meditating and reflecting on their experiences. When you practise reflective meditation, you may have a deeper understanding of life and what it's all about. Reflective meditation can help you see things more clearly. You now have a heightened awareness of both your surroundings and your own life, as well as an increased social consciousness. You may also use reflective meditation to assist you in locating internal issues and working through them.

Meditation that Is Focused on the Heart

The fifth primary kind of meditation is known as meditation with the focus on the heart. This kind of meditation involves the use of practises that help you awaken your innate capacity for love and compassion. You will become kinder, nicer, and more loving after you have successfully mastered this form of meditation and can call it your own. You will be more empathetic towards other people's predicaments and more forgiving of those who have wronged you. You will have the ability to think on your life in a creative manner and to listen intently to the words that other people have to say as they are said.

There are advantages to be gained by practising any kind of meditation. However, if you want to get rid of stress, it is probably reasonable to say that concentration meditation gives the greatest set of advantages. Determining which style of meditation works best for your requirements is totally up to you, but it is safe to say that concentration meditation offers the greatest collection of benefits. Through the practise of meditation, one is able to transcend their regular condition and satisfy their most inner goals and wants. You may take control of your thoughts and the way you see the world around you via the practise of meditation. If you practise meditation on a consistent basis, it will unquestionably assist you in figuring out what the real purpose of life is. You won't have to worry about experiencing stress anymore, at least not to the same degree as you formerly did.

Your life can be transformed by meditation, but only if you are prepared to open yourself up to such transformations. Try some meditation if you've ever been curious about what it might be like to have an experience of being outside of your body. It is a great sense of mental happiness, and before you realise it, you will be in a continual state of serenity rather than tension. You may achieve this state of mental bliss by practising mindfulness.

How To Deepen Your Spirituality Through Meditation And Mindfulness Practises In Order To Draw Nearer To Your Creator

Increased spirituality is only one of the several advantages that comes with regular meditation practise. When you cultivate awareness, focus, and meditation on a consistent basis, you bring yourself into closer alignment with the Divine and the Creator.

You may develop a closer relationship with the one who created you by doing the following meditation technique:

Place yourself in a posture that is comfortable and shut your eyes.

Take a few slow, deep breaths and be sure to exhale through your mouth rather than your nose.

Invoke the presence of the Creator by offering a brief prayer of thanksgiving.

While you are breathing in and out, repeat the word "God" to yourself. In the event that your thoughts start to wander, return your attention back to the word "God." Continue doing this for ten to fifteen minutes.

Your time spent meditating should end with a brief expression of thanks in the form of a prayer.

This should be done every day.

It is important to keep in mind that one of the most common types of meditation is prayer. When you pray to the Divine and the Creator, avoid using a pattern, and don't make any requests for specific items. Make sure that your prayer has a conversational tenor to it. You will feel more connected to the Divine Power as you engage in this practise.

Meditation is one of the many practises that might bring a person closer to the Divine. Another kind of meditation is called mindfulness. When you practise mindfulness and you live in the present now, you have the opportunity to notice things that you have taken for granted in the past, such as the air that you breathe, the lovely flowers that are growing in your yard, and the other things and people that you are blessed with. When you cultivate mindfulness and focus on being present in the moment, you more often find yourself awestruck by the incredible work of the creator, and as a consequence, you feel a stronger connection to the Divine.

Advice On How To Calm Your Mind And Take Pleasure In Living In The Here And Now

In addition to the traditional practise of meditating while sitting, there are various methods and approaches that, when added to your meditation routine, may assist you in calming your mind and just being present in the moment. The following are some suggestions that might help you learn to still your thoughts and focus on the here and now.

Walking meditation is a kind of mindfulness practise that combines physical movement with concentration on the present moment. When you practise walking meditation, you concentrate on your breath and your steps, taking a few moments here and there to take in and take pleasure in the scenery. Meditation while walking is a powerful practise for quieting the mind and releasing all of its mental chatter and anxieties. It encourages you to be present in the here and now.

Develop a close relationship with your ideas and communicate with them - The majority of us just let our thoughts to pass through our heads unnoticed because we haven't taken the time to get to know them. As a direct consequence of this, your mind is always racing with anxious and negative ideas. Take conscious note of your ideas. Create space in your schedule every day to sit quietly, concentrate on your breathing, and put into practise some of the fundamental mindfulness methods that we covered in the s that came before this one. Whenever a thought crosses your mind, just acknowledge it without passing judgement on it, and then return your attention back to the breath.

Take Mental Breaks - While you are at work or school each day, make sure you give yourself some time to clear your head, relax, and rest your mind by giving yourself some mental breaks. During your lunch break, give yourself some time to just sit at your desk and do nothing, or take a stroll about the neighbourhood for a few minutes.

Stop thinking is one of the most difficult techniques for calming the mind; it involves fully emptying one's thoughts from one's head. This indicates that one must suppress an idea in order to prevent it from entering the mind. It also implies that you should constantly edit your ideas in order to avoid being controlled by your thoughts.People who have developed great mental power via the consistent practise of meditation are the only ones who are capable of using this method.

Do not go through life acting as though you are merely going through the motions. Try not to live in the past or let your worries about the future consume you. The only way to really appreciate the present is to train your thoughts to be still.

Things That Should Be Kept In Mind When Teaching Mindfulness

Although the practise of mindfulness and the related exercises are intended to have a soothing impact on everyone concerned, it may be challenging to teach the mindful activities and to incorporate these exercises into daily routines. However, professionals in the field of mindfulness have provided seven suggestions or considerations that should be kept in mind while beginning the path of mindfulness with your kid.

Make an Effort to Reduce Distractions

The first piece of advice is one that is applicable to the establishment of any kind of bedtime routine with your kid, regardless of whether or not you are attempting to use mindfulness habits. As suggested by Moralis (2016), you should make an effort to cut down on the number of things that might divert your attention throughout the nightly routine.

Your youngster is exposed to a wide variety of forms of stimulus during the course of a typical day. As a consequence of this, it may be challenging for individuals to detach themselves from the many forms of stimulation. Because of this, it is imperative that you take responsibility, restrict the distractions that they are exposed to, and ultimately enforce the separation. This can be turning off the television and any other electronic devices a certain length of time before night or turning down the lights in the home before going to bed.

Repeat the Actions That Are Preferred

Another tip that might help you construct a good nighttime routine is to model the behaviour that you want your child to exhibit. It will be useful for your kid to witness you become peaceful, especially if you want them to quiet down, and if you want them to see you get calm. It would be helpful for children to see you also engaging in the activities associated with the nighttime ritual, such as turning off the television, getting into pyjamas, and reading books.

Mirroring and embodying the desired behaviour will show the kid that you respect them and will help them comprehend the stages of the routine (Moralis, 2016). Although it may seem unfair that you are the adult and they are the child, this will show the child that you respect them.

Maintain a Consistency

Being consistent is one of the most important aspects of building a routine, and this is true whether you are attempting to construct a new fitness programme for yourself or want to see effects from a new diet that you have started. In the process of formulating a nighttime routine for children, it is also an essential consideration. According to Moralis (2016), being persistent increases the likelihood that you will experience the outcomes you seek more quickly.

There are going to be a few one-off evenings in which the normal schedule will be altered or thrown totally out the window. On the other hand, the fact that there is no set pattern to follow before night shouldn't be the thing that is reliable about bedtime. On the evenings in which the child's normal schedule deviates, you are obligated to provide an explanation for the deviation, such as the fact that a special event is taking place that night or that there are guests staying at the home.

Take Everything One Step at a Time

The journey of incorporating mindfulness into the habit of going to bed, as well as the process of building such a routine, should ideally be broken down into manageable phases. If you suddenly change the routine you use to put the kid to bed, it will be quite perplexing for them. It will also raise the likelihood that they will not behave appropriately, which will, in turn, produce the general irritation that is involved with attempting to adopt a nighttime routine (Moralis, 2016).

You may want to begin by eliminating all of the potential distractions in the area where you sleep. After that, you can gradually include a variety of activities that involve mindfulness and meditation into your nightly routine. As a result of your actions, not only will there be a greater possibility that the kid will remember the evening routine, but there will also be a greater possibility that the mindfulness exercises will have the desired results for you.

Don't Put Too Much Effort Into It

In addition to approaching the trip in stages, it is important to avoid exerting undue pressure on certain behaviours. When you force your kid to engage in certain behaviours, they may start to experience an unpleasant feeling of urgency inside themselves. They could be afraid of the behaviour since they don't comprehend the reasoning behind why it's being requested of them (Moralis, 2016).

Because of this, it is recommended that you not only break the process down into manageable chunks, but also that you try not to take the behaviour too seriously. Comfort the youngster and reassure them that it is all right that they did not do what they were asked the first time and that it is alright if they did not execute the activity or display the behaviour as soon as you asked them to. Explain to them why it is vital to behave in a certain way and tell them that you will try again the following night. If you remove some of the pressure off the youngster, they will be more eager to do the behaviour when you ask them to. They will not have the impression that they are being coerced into doing it; rather, they will have the impression that they are voluntarily behaving in an appropriate manner.

Have Patience!

Being patient is a trait that will serve you well in many aspects of parenting, including the routine of putting your children to bed at night. Your kid is not only acquiring new behaviours, but they are also attempting to adjust to the shift in the pattern that they follow before going to bed. Consider how successfully teenagers and adults adapt to new situations. Change is something that is generally met with resistance from the majority of people. However, it may be more challenging for youngsters since they may not yet have the communication skills necessary to comprehend why the shift is taking place and why it is significant. According to Moralis (2016), developing a patient disposition is one of the most important skills that can be honed in order to become proficient in the execution of the nightly routine in general as well as the use of various mindful approaches.

Have Some Fun This is the last piece of advice we want to share with you as you go on the road of mindfulness with your kid or children: make sure you have some fun! The path towards mindfulness and a more tranquil state of being is intended to be one that is one that is both entertaining and thrilling. Stress reduction and mental clarity are the goals of the practise of mindfulness meditation. They are not intended to cause more stress, nor are they intended to aggravate existing levels of tension or frustration. Because of this, it is recommended that you make the bedtime ritual something pleasurable to look forward to. be some jokes, and be sure to laugh quite a bit. If the kid notices that you take pleasure in the many stages and activities that are a part of the routine, it increases the likelihood that the child will continue with the various activities and take pleasure in them themselves (Moralis, 2016).

When a person is content and unruffled, practising mindfulness and meditation yields better benefits than when they are neither of those things.

* * *

It is time to learn these various mindfulness exercises now that we have discussed what mindfulness is and its advantages, why getting a good night's sleep is crucial, and some advice to aid you along your path.

Chakra Of The Solar Plexus

Ego operating on a higher level is connected to the solar plexus chakra, which is located in the middle of the body. This involves having confidence in oneself, having a feeling of purpose in one's job, and accepting responsibility for one's actions. You are able to take responsibility for your life and act with self-confidence and self-discipline when your root, sacral, and solar plexus chakras are all balanced and open. Yellow is the colour that represents the solar plexus chakra, which is located in the middle of the body. It may be found slightly above the navel and under the rib cage in this position.

Chakra del Corazon

Love, empathy, tolerance, and acceptance are all emotions that are connected with the heart chakra. This has nothing to do with just platonic love, despite the fact that romantic love is inextricably linked to the heart chakra. The heart chakra is the source of all forms of love, including love for oneself as well as acceptance of oneself. Green is the colour associated with the heart chakra; nevertheless, stones and crystals that are pink in colour are equally effective when used for mending the heart chakra. The location of the heart chakra is directly in the middle of the chest.

Chakra de la Throat

The region at the bottom of the neck is the location of the first spiritual chakra, which is called the throat chakra. The throat chakra is associated with communication and being honest, as you would have guessed based on its location. The throat chakra is represented by the colour blue.

The Chakra of the Third Eye

The third eye chakra may be found in the forehead area, exactly in the middle, and it is situated just over the actual eyes. In addition to this, it has been linked to a gland located in the brain known as the pineal gland. Since ancient times, it has been widely accepted that the third eye serves as a portal through which we may see the intuitive and psychic worlds. Consequently, this is a "eye" that perceives information from realms of reality that are not physical. If one's third eye is closed, one cannot utilise their intuitive talents; nonetheless, we all possess these abilities. To your relief, it is both feasible and desirable to repair and open your third eye chakra. This chakra has a great deal of vitality. Indigo is the colour that corresponds to the third eye chakra in the body.

The top, or crown, chakra

The crown chakra may either be found at the very top of the head or, as some authorities have hypothesised, it can also be found somewhat above the very top of the head. It has a very intimate connection to the brain and the rest of the nervous system. Consciousness and awareness are connected with the crown chakra since this is the crown chakra's most fundamental function. However, it is much more than that since the crown chakra represents the connection between us and our higher selves as well as our spirituality. It is connected to the concepts of presence and happiness as well as knowledge. The crown chakra is related, on the most basic level, with communication with higher states of existence and the spiritual oneness of the cosmos. Purple is the primary colour linked with the crown chakra; however, white and gold are also connected with this chakra.

www.ingramcontent.com/pod-product-compliance
Lightning Source LLC
Chambersburg PA
CBHW050357120526
44590CB00015B/1729